Ultimate Guide To the Roswell UFO Crash

A Tour of Roswell's UFO Landmarks

4th Edition

By Noe Torres
Photographs by E. J. Wilson

RoswellBooks.com

Edinburg, Texas

4th Edition

ISBN: 978-1-7342523-0-9

Printed in the United States of America

"Modern UFO sightings really began with the Roswell incident in 1947, when a crashed craft containing the corpses of several aliens was found in Roswell, New Mexico. Make no mistake, Roswell happened. I've seen secret files which show the government knew about it - but decided not to tell the public. There were very good security reasons for not informing the public about Roswell. Quite simply, we wouldn't have known how to deal with the technology of intelligent beings advanced enough to send a craft to Earth. The world would have panicked if we'd known aliens were visiting us."

Dr. Edgar Mitchell (1930-2016), legendary NASA astronaut, from a 1998 interview with British reporter John Earls.

Astronaut Edgar Mitchell

To our friends, Ruben Uriarte and John LeMay, with whom we have wandered the desolate places of the Earth.

CONTENTS

FOREWORD
By Jesse Marcel, Jr.

Shortly after taking part in the Bikini Atoll atomic bomb tests in July of 1946, my father was assigned to the Roswell Army Air Field (RAAF), the home base for the 509th Composite Bomb Group, which had ended World War II with the atomic bombing of Japan. He was Major Jesse A. Marcel, the intelligence officer for the 509th, and he had been on the "inside" of the top-secret mission that brought the war with Japan to a close. His military training and experience were extensive, and his role as intelligence officer for the only atomic bomb group in the world was a serious one. Anyone who suggests that my dad wouldn't have been able to identify a downed high-altitude balloon is completely ignorant of his background and his training.

In late 1946, my parents and I moved into RAAF base housing, and, since the base had no school facilities at that time, I attended Mountain View School, located just outside the base, on the way into Roswell. A few months later, in the spring of 1947, we moved into town to a corner lot house located at 1300 West Seventh Street, which looks pretty much the same today as it did all those many years ago. There is a vacant lot still there across the street adjacent to the house where Johnny Peck, one of my close friends, lived. Those spring and early summer days in Roswell were the best times of my life. Gayle Salee, Johnny Peck and I spent many hours bicycling all over Roswell and west into the desert. I have such fond memories of that time of my life, especially the many hours spent playing with friends during the long, hot Roswell summers.

My dad had an office at the Roswell Army Air Field, but he really did not keep regular office hours there, as his job duties routinely required that he work far beyond normal working hours, including nights and weekends. The only time I ever saw where he worked at the RAAF was when he took my mom and me on a tour. What I remember most is a large room where briefing sessions were held for the bomb crews. In that room, I recall seeing

1

a world map that glowed in luminescent hues from ultraviolet lights. All of this was quite impressive to me at the time.

Jesse Marcel, Jr., 2008 Photo (Courtesy of Colonel Marcel)

Things went along routinely for the first part of 1947. And then "it" happened. One night in early July, I recall that my dad did not come home for supper, or if he did, I did not see him. Something seemed odd. I did not see him again until very late the next evening or perhaps even very early in the morning on the day after that. At any rate, when he finally came home, I was asleep in my room and had already been asleep for hours, exhausted from a full day of bicycling with my friends.

I recall my dad waking me up in the middle of the night. He led me into the kitchen where, I think, my mother was already up and looking at a lot of debris scattered on the kitchen floor. Dad was very excited at what was there, but honestly, I could not understand what all his excitement was about. To me, the junk strewn on the kitchen floor was just a lot of metal fragments that looked like a foil mixed together with something that seemed to be black plastic and also some metallic-looking beams.

2

While the debris did not make a great impression on me at first, my dad's description of it most certainly did. He told my mother and me that what we were looking at were parts from a flying saucer. Although, still groggy with sleep, the full implications of the phrase "flying saucer" did not sink it at first, I realized from my dad's excited state that this was something extremely unique and important.

My interest was especially piqued when Dad said that I would never see something like this again in my life. The realization suddenly dawned on me that what he was saying is that what we were looking at had come from somewhere besides Earth and that this was part of a machine from another planet.

He instructed us to search very carefully through the wreckage looking for any familiar electronic components, such as vacuum tubes, resistors condensers or wire. In fact, he had already searched the debris for these types of components and had found none, but he wanted us to conduct our own search and satisfy our own curiosities. So, Mom and I dutifully complied with his request and found nothing that looked like conventional electronics in the debris.

Regarding the thin metallic debris that looked like foil, I recall that it seemed similar to today's aluminum wrap, and yet there was a noticeable difference in its appearance and feel. I struggle to adequately explain the exact differences and can only say that it seemed like aluminum wrap but clearly was not.

The strangest parts of the debris were some straight metallic pieces that I have always thought of as I-beams. Marked on one surface of these beams were strange hieroglyphic-like symbols with kind of a violet or purple hue to them. One of these I-beams was 12 to 18 inches long and about three eighths of an inch across (cross sectional width). The beam appeared to be metallic and may have been made of the same material as the foil.

The other material in the debris seemed to be kind of a black plastic, sort of like Bakelite, which was a common material used in the manufacture of countertops at that time. Upon examining this dark material, along with the foil-like material and the I-beams, I was left with the distinct impression that the debris was something very special and certainly not of any common or ordinary composition. My father made clear to us that we might never see anything like it again in our lives.

People often ask me, "Why didn't you keep some of it?" The reason, as simple as it sounds, is that the viewing of the material had been a privilege granted to me by my father, and I knew that his job demanded that he take it the RAAF. The material was not ours to keep and was ultimately the property of the United States Army Air Force. In truth, it never occurred to me to keep any of it, and I guarantee that had I kept any of it, I would not have it now because the military was hell-bent on recovering all of it. First, the army worked to ensure that none of the material fell into civilian hands, and second, if any of it did, they used every resource at their disposal to get it back.

Bill Brazel held on to a piece of the strange debris for some time after the Roswell Incident, but shortly after he spoke of it to some of his friends, he received a visit from a group of mysterious individuals presumably representing military intelligence, and the debris was taken from him. That was a clear example of how hard it was to hold on to any of it.

I'm often asked how this experience affected my life. In other words, how did I change after handling material which to this day I am convinced came from another civilization? The experience was definitely a "game changer" in my life. An immediate impact was that it increased my belief in God as Creator of the nearly limitless universe. Suddenly and profoundly, I realized that human beings are *not alone* in the vast cosmos and that God's unbounded creative energies did not begin or end with the creation of life on Earth. After what I witnessed in Roswell, I attended Saint Peter's Roman Catholic School, where I sought out a personal faith that could sustain me and could help me understand my role in the immensity of God's universe.

Hand in hand with my renewed spiritual leanings, I also developed a keen interest in astronomy and read all I could about other star systems. Although it would be 50 years before astronomers confirmed the existence of other planetary systems, my family and I already knew the truth back in 1947. Obviously, the wreckage we handled in the kitchen of our small home came from a civilization not of the Earth.

Colonel Jesse Marcel, Jr. in 2004 While Serving as Flight Surgeon for the 189th Attack Helicopter Battalion in Iraq (Courtesy of Colonel Marcel)

Evidence exists that ancient humans saw UFOs flying across the sky and depicted such sightings in primitive drawings, paintings, sculpture, and other media. From crude drawings in caves showing flying disks in the sky to medieval paintings containing flying saucers hovering in the background, the images are haunting. Fast forward to modern times and the Roswell Incident is the "grandfather" of all UFO events. It was the trigger for the world's fascination with unknown aerial phenomena, which continues unabated to this very day. Since there was physical evidence in the form of debris falling on the Foster Ranch, the Roswell crash was hard to cover up. In spite of official denials by the military stating that the debris was merely a crashed weather balloon, interest in the Roswell case continues to grow even today, despite the passing of decades.

Why do so many people all around the world remain fascinated by this case? I believe it is the one case with a preponderance of unyielding evidence. There were just too many first-hand witnesses attesting to the fact that the Roswell Incident was something of far greater significance than a weather balloon. Witnesses have given sworn statements that, after the crash, they saw some really exotic materials and, even, the remains of a crew.

Although we may not know exactly how the truth will finally be revealed, we can be confident that it will be. We can also rest assured that intelligent life does exist elsewhere in the universe and that we have been visited. These facts are inescapable.

Allow this book that you now hold in your hands to be your guide on an amazing journey to all the key places that are connected to the events of the Roswell UFO crash of 1947. Here you will read about my former home, which still stands in Roswell and where we examined the strange wreckage. You will also read about many other places, including the mysterious RAAF aircraft hangar, where witnesses say UFO wreckage and bodies were temporarily stored. Through a clearer understanding of the Roswell event, we discover greater truth about the universe and our place in it. *WE ARE NOT ALONE.*

Jesse Marcel, Jr.
Helena, Montana

Author's Note: Sadly, Jesse Marcel, Jr. passed away in April 2013 at his home in Montana. We will miss him greatly. To the very end, he staunchly held the belief that he had touched and handled debris from an extraterrestrial spacecraft.

🛸 INTRODUCTION

The objective of this book is simple - to transport the reader on a self-guided tour of modern-day Roswell, visiting the very places where the Roswell Incident happened. It puts the power of discovery into your hands, allowing you to explore the tangible in order to experience the intangible. In this revised edition, we have even included global positioning system (GPS) coordinates for all the sites we discuss in the book, and we have included a quick response (QR) barcode at the start of every chapter, as in the example shown here. When scanned with a smart phone, tablet computer, or other Internet-connected device, the barcode will load up the exact location of each site and display it on the Google Maps ™ web site. Look for the green arrow pointer.

With these wonderful new tools in hand, be prepared for the mind-blowing experience of visiting the places where the actual events of Roswell Incident took place. Walking the same sidewalks where the witnesses walked. Standing in the same rooms where witnesses said they saw alien bodies. Looking across the same rocky field where metallic pieces of something strange came raining down out of the sky. In visiting these wondrous places, you encounter an overwhelming "presence" – call it the force of history or call it the paranormal. You will find yourself face to face with what is potentially one of the most monumental moments in human history, if we are to believe the hundreds of individuals who have claimed involvement in the case.

This book is organized in the form of a self-guided driving tour with stops along the way, beginning in the downtown section of Roswell and then slowly moving outward to more distant sites, to neighboring towns and ranches, and even to nearby cities and counties. The book's starting point, downtown Roswell, is a natural one, considering that most of the mystery and intrigue surrounding this case happened in and around the city limits. Also, since most of the sites of interest are located in Roswell, it is the ideal base of operations, from which readers may venture out to explore other more distant sites.

Our stops include the army air base hospital where witnesses say strange bodies, not quite human, were brought in from a UFO crash site in the desert north of Roswell. Other stops include a section of a former ranch where witnesses in 1947 found a field of metallic debris with reported unearthly properties. Another stop is a cafeteria where a nearly hysterical nurse drew sketches of strange creatures she saw being autopsied by military doctors. And, our stops also include other stretches of desert ranchland north of Roswell where witnesses stumbled upon additional UFO evidence.

These are but a few of the wonders that await us, as we take an incredible journey back to the year 1947 and experience first-hand what it must have been like for the people of Roswell who suddenly gained awareness that, in the blink of an eye, beings from somewhere other than Earth might have landed right in their midst.

It is now time to embark on a wondrous journey back in time and down the rabbit hole with Alice. Whether you are actually using this book to take a self-guided tour of all the locations mentioned or whether you are using it merely to take a virtual tour in your own mind, please be advised that when you clamber back aboveground after wandering around in this rabbit hole, your view of life and the universe may never be the same ....

ONE:
MARCEL RESIDENCE

Status: Still standing.
Location: 1300 W. 7th St. (Intersection of W. 7th & Montana Ave.)
Accessibility: Private residence.
GPS Coordinates: 33.399624, -104.540473.

In the early morning hours of July 8, 1947, Jesse Marcel, Jr., age 11, was asleep in his bedroom at 1300 West 7th Street, when his father suddenly came into his room and excitedly told him to follow him into the kitchen to look at something very strange. What Major Jesse Marcel, Sr. was about to show his son on that quiet summer evening would change both their lives forever. After the two walked through the quiet house in eager anticipation, the elder Marcel spread out on the kitchen table a boxful of metallic debris like neither had ever seen before.

East Side of Former Marcel Residence at 1300 W. 7th (Photo by E.J. Wilson)

The material, collected by the elder Marcel earlier in the day at the Foster Ranch, north of town, included metal foil, broken pieces of a plastic-like material, and metal beams ("I" beams). "The foil had a more or less dull appearance, kind of like a burnished aluminum surface, not shiny or highly reflective, although one side may have been more polished than the other," Jesse Marcel, Jr. wrote in his book *The Roswell Legacy*. "The surface of the foil itself was somewhat smooth. The pieces themselves didn't have any distinct design or shape; they were amorphous. I remember looking at some of the foil material for quite a while. In particular, I remember how light it was – if you dropped it, it would float like a feather."

MAJOR JESSE A. MARCELL
S-2
1946 RAAF Yearbook Photo (Courtesy of HSSNM)

When Major Marcel later examined the material back at the Roswell Army Air Field, he noticed that when he bent or folded a piece of the strange foil, it would immediately straighten itself and return to its original shape, a property that caused UFO researchers to refer to it as "memory metal." Additionally, attempts to dent or deform some of the larger pieces of the debris using a sledgehammer were unsuccessful, which meant that some of the pieces were virtually indestructible.

But perhaps the strangest thing witnessed at the Marcel residence that night in 1947 was a group of strange hieroglyphic-like symbols on one of the pieces of the debris. In *The Roswell Legacy*, Marcel, Jr. remembered, "There were about thirty symbols, one right after another. These figures were solid; they were not line drawings.... One reminded me of a seal balancing a ball on its nose. The symbol was like a truncated pyramid with a solid ball over the apex ... The symbol located just to the right of this was an oblate spheroid. The spheroid sometimes would appear with two smaller spheroids below the larger spheroid, sometimes above. As I recall the next symbol had the same configuration, but it was reversed 90 degrees. To the right of these symbols was a simple oval...."

After the impromptu viewing of the flying saucer crash debris, Major Marcel gathered up all the material and took it with him back to the base. As it turned out, he later accompanied some of the material collected from the Foster Ranch as it was flown to Wright Air Field at Dayton, Ohio, aboard a military cargo plane.

"When my dad returned to Roswell [from Dayton, Ohio], he cautioned my mother and me never to tell others what we had seen that night. In talking with him later, he confirmed that this material was from an unearthly craft, and I was certainly convinced of it myself."

North Side of Former Marcel Residence. Window on Right was Jesse Marcel, Jr.'s Bedroom (Photo by E.J. Wilson)

Contrary to what some people believe, the Marcel residence was never "ransacked" or even searched by military officials looking for pieces of the Foster Ranch debris that may have been left behind. Jesse Marcel, Jr. said, "No, I don't recall any military people coming to the house after that night [when Major Marcel showed the debris to his wife and son]. I think that my dad as being the intelligence officer for the 509th had enough credibility that they felt there was no need to come to the house and look for any 'spare parts.' I can safely say that no one from the military came over at any time to look around."

BLM Map Showing Location of Former Marcel Residence

Today, as we stand outside the former residence of the Marcels on West 7th Street in Roswell, we can only imagine what it must have been like during that moment forever frozen in time when the tiny kitchen table of the house held fragments of what may have been a spacecraft from beyond Earth. In our mind's eye, we can see 11-year-old Jesse Marcel, Jr. holding the wreckage in his hands and wondering about humanity's place in the universe. "From that evening on, my life took on a different meaning," he wrote in *The Roswell Legacy*. "I could never look at the night sky the same way again, because, for all I knew, someone else might be looking back."

The former Marcel residence is located on the southwest corner of the intersection of West 7th Street and Montana Avenue. Across the street to the north is an empty lot, which was there in 1947. Jesse Marcel, Jr. remembers playing in that empty lot with neighborhood friends. "Johnny Peck, Gale Salee and I played war games and rode our bicycles on that lot," Marcel said. His friend Johnny Peck lived in the house just north of the vacant lot.

When visiting the former Marcel residence in Roswell, please respect the privacy and property of the home's current occupants. You can drive by and take pictures from the street, but please do not trespass.

TWO:
WILMOT RESIDENCE

Status: Still standing.
Location: 105 S. Pennsylvania Ave. (Intersection of 1st & Penn.)
Accessibility: Private residence.
GPS Coordinates: 33.392694, -104.525994.

Our extraordinary tour continues with a downtown Roswell home where a strange object was seen flying across the western horizon on the evening of July 2, 1947. At first glance, this UFO sighting seemed of no more significance than any of the hundreds of others. But what made this sighting unique in retrospect is that it served as a harbinger of things to come. It was the first indication that something beyond any earthly explanation was about to descend upon the quiet desert community of Roswell.

The Former Wilmot Residence (Photo by E.J. Wilson)

With an estimated 1947 population of 22,000, Roswell's economic lifeblood came mainly from two industries: ranching and the Roswell Army Air Field on the south end of town. Many of the town's businesses were geared toward providing goods and services to the soldiers stationed at the base. There is little doubt that Dan Wilmot, owner of the Wilmot Hardware Store, also benefited greatly from the presence of the Army base.

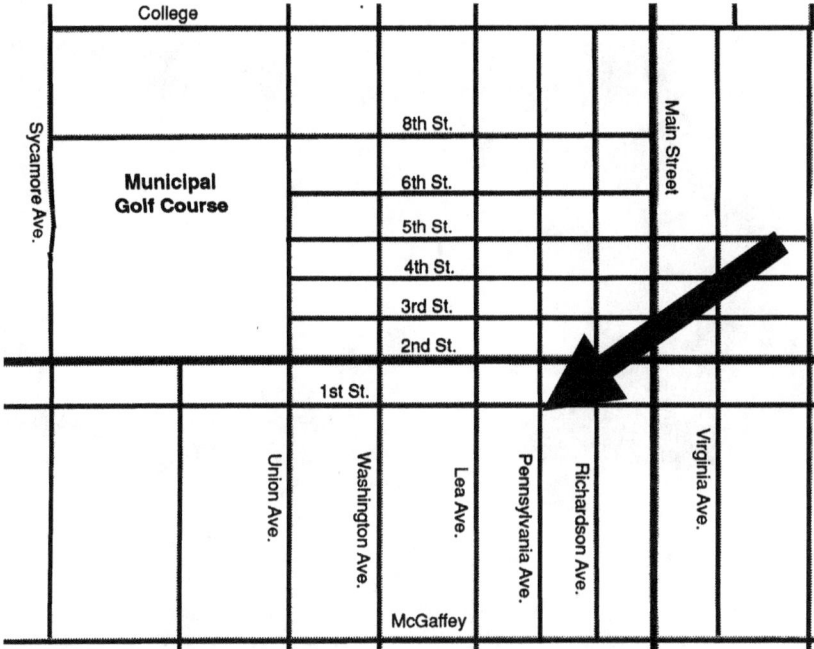

Former Wilmot Home at Corner of 1ˢᵗ Street and S. Pennsylvania Ave.

On that quiet summer evening, Wilmot and his wife were sitting on the front porch of their home at 105 South Pennsylvania Avenue in the heart of downtown, when they saw a brightly-lit, circular "flying disk" streaking across the sky over the western part of town. In the story of their sighting, published six days later in the Roswell newspaper, they described a "large glowing object" approaching their position from the southeast and moving toward the northwest at a high rate of speed.

Wilmot told the newspaper that the object seemed to be flying at an altitude of about 1,500 feet and traveling between 400 and

500 miles per hour. He estimated that the object may have been between 15 and 20 feet in diameter. Wilmot and his wife stood in their yard and viewed the UFO for slightly less than one minute, before it disappeared over the treetops off to the west at Six Mile Hill, a 10-mile long rocky ridge that forms the city's western boundary. Wilmot heard no sound at all during the sighting, but his wife thought she heard a very faint and very brief "swishing" sound as the object moved past their vantage point.

1940s Photo of Main Street with Wilmot Hardware Sign Visible on Upper Right (Courtesy of the Historical Society for Southeast New Mexico)

The newspaper account stated, "… it [the UFO] looked oval in shape like two inverted saucers, faced mouth to mouth, or like two old type washbowls placed, together in the same fashion. The entire body glowed as though light were showing through from inside, though not like it would be if a light were merely underneath."

16

The newspaper article concluded by saying, "Wilmot, who is one of the most respected and reliable citizens in town, kept the story to himself hoping that someone else would come out and tell about having seen one, but finally today [July 8] decided that he would go ahead and tell about it. The announcement that the RAAF [Roswell Army Air Field] was in possession of one came only a few minutes after he decided to release the details of what he had seen."

Interestingly, the newspaper reporter felt it was important to state that the Wilmots disclosed their sighting "a few minutes" before the famous press release by the Roswell Army Air Field stating that the U.S. Army had captured a flying saucer.

The complete story of the Wilmots' sighting, as reported in the *Roswell Record* on July 8, 1947, follows:

"Mr. and Mrs. Dan Wilmot apparently were the only persons in Roswell who saw what they thought was a flying disk. They were sitting on their porch at 105 South Penn. last Wednesday night at about ten o'clock when a large glowing object zoomed out of the sky from the southeast, going in a northwesterly direction at a high rate of speed. Wilmot called Mrs. Wilmot's attention to it and both ran down into the yard to watch.

"It was in sight less than a minute, perhaps 40 or 50 seconds, Wilmot estimated. Wilmot said that it appeared to him to be about 1,500 feet high and going fast. He estimated between 400 and 500 miles per hour.

"In appearance it looked oval in shape like two inverted saucers, faced mouth to mouth, or like two old type washbowls placed, together in the same fashion. The entire body glowed as though light were showing through from inside, though not like it would be if a light were merely underneath. From where he stood Wilmot said that the object looked to be about 5 feet in size, and making allowance for the distance it was from town he figured that it must have been 15 to 20 feet in diameter, though this was just a guess. Wilmot said that he heard no sound but that Mrs. Wilmot said she heard a swishing sound for a very short time. The object came into view from the southeast and disappeared over the treetops in the general vicinity of Six Mile Hill.

"Wilmot, who is one of the most respected and reliable citizens in town, kept the story to himself hoping that someone else would come out and tell about having seen one, but finally today decided that he would go ahead and tell about it. The announcement that the RAAF was in possession of one came only a few minutes after he decided to release the details of what he had seen."

The former Wilmot residence at 105 South Pennsylvania Avenue still exists as a private residence and home-based business (dog grooming service). Visitors are urged to respect the current homeowners' property and privacy. Please do not trespass or disturb the current occupants.

THREE:
ROSWELL FIRE
STATION

Status: Original building demolished. Current fire station built on same site.
Location: 200 South Richardson Avenue
Accessibility: City government building.
GPS Coordinates: 33.391772, -104.524501.

The involvement of the Roswell fire department in the 1947 UFO incident was first revealed by Frankie Rowe, daughter of firefighter Dan Dwyer, who told her that he had seen a crashed UFO and bodies. This incredible story began early on the morning of July 5, 1947, when the Roswell fire station at 200 South Richardson first received word about an "incident" out north of town.

Roswell's Central Fire Station is Located on Site of 1947 Station
(Photo by E.J. Wilson)

The crash site Dwyer said he visited was not at the Foster Ranch, where Major Marcel gathered the debris that he showed to his wife and son. Rather, this was a distinctly different location, some miles away. Researchers believe that the same UFO that scattered debris over the Foster Ranch remained airborne for a while longer before crashing at a location closer to the town of Roswell. This "final" crash site is said to be where the main section of the UFO came to rest and where bodies were recovered.

Fireman Dan Dwyer also saw a small non-human creature standing outside the crashed saucer, according to his daughter Frankie Rowe, who was 12 years old in 1947. Rowe said, "Daddy was on the crew that went. He told us later that what he saw was the wreckage of some type of flying craft. He did not know what it looked like. He couldn't tell. He said they were very small pieces. A lot of it had been picked up."

"There were apparently three people in the craft, because he saw two body bags and he saw one live person, a very small being about the size of a 10-year-old child," Rowe remembers. "They put this being in a vehicle and took it away immediately.... They did take the two body bags away in a separate vehicle." (Randle & Schmitt, pp. 20-21)

Left: Photo of Jerusalem Cricket (Wikipedia.org)
Right: Alleged Gray Alien (Courtesy of Bob Dean)

According to Rowe, her father believed the strange being he saw standing near the wreckage was definitely an adult, although its body was small. The being was completely hairless, and it seemed uninjured. In struggling to describe it, Dwyer compared its face to that of an insect called the Jerusalem Cricket or "Child of the Earth." This insect, which is common in the Southwestern U.S., is said to resemble the so-called "gray" aliens.

Rowe herself later had a chance to see some of the extraordinary debris that had been recovered where the object crashed. "I was in the fire house waiting for my father to take me home. A state trooper arrived and displayed a piece of metallic debris that he said he'd picked up on the crash site. It was a dull gray and about the thickness of aluminum foil. When wadded into a ball, it would unfold itself. The fire fighters were unable to cut or burn it." [Randle & Schmitt, p. 263]

Another View of Roswell's Central Fire Station (Photo by E.J. Wilson)

In an interview with investigator Karl Pflock, Rowe said, "[The state trooper] took his hand out of his pocket, and he dropped what he had in his fist on the table. He said it was something he picked up out at the crash site. It looked like quicksilver when it was on the table, but you could wad it up. [It was] a little larger than . . . [his] hand. It had jagged edges [and it was a dull grayish-silver color.] You couldn't feel it in your hand. It was so

21

thin that it felt like holding a hair . . . It wasn't anything you'd ever seen before. It flowed like quicksilver when you laid it on the table. [The firemen and the trooper] tried to tear it, cut it and burn it. It wadded up into nothing. The state cop said he'd gotten away with just this one small piece, and he said he didn't know how long he'd be able to keep it, if the military found out."

A member of the military later came to Frankie Rowe's house and told her, in the presence of her mother, that if she ever spoke to anyone about the unusual piece of metal, she would simply "be taken out into the desert, never to return." [Randle & Schmitt, p. 263]

In an account appearing on *ufocon.blogspot.com* in March 2009, UFO investigator Anthony Bragalia told of his conversation with the son of the late Rue Chrisman, who was the Roswell Fire Chief in 1947. After much prodding by Bragalia, the younger Chrisman finally admitted, "It did happen. There was a big cover up. The crash was real." When Bragalia asked why he believed it, Chrisman responded, "I knew too many who knew."

Then Chrisman gave Bragalia the name of the only Roswell firefighter from 1947 that was still alive (at age 90) in 2009, identified only as "Mr. Smith," in order to protect his privacy. Smith told Bragalia that immediately after the UFO crash, an intimidating Army Colonel visited the Roswell Fire Department. The colonel told the firemen that an "unknown object from someplace else" had crashed in the desert outside Roswell and warned them to keep the matter secret and not to attempt to visit the crash scene. He told them that the rescue operation that was being handled entirely by the military." Because of what the colonel said to them and also what he later heard from other witnesses, Smith is convinced that the crashed object was not from the Earth.

Smith also confirmed Frankie Rowe's story that Dan Dwyer and several other firefighters went out to the crash site, despite the colonel's directive. According to Smith, the city firemen went of their own volition, and not really in response to a "call." It was actually the Roswell Army Air Field's own fire department that was heavily involved in the crash recovery and clean-up process,

Smith said. The RAAF firefighters were the ones who "knew the most" about what happened.

Smith also told Bragalia that the Roswell City Manager in 1947, C.M. Woodbury, later visited the fire department and, in a very forceful manner, ordered all firefighters to say absolutely nothing about the UFO crash north of town. Woodbury, according to Bragalia's research, was a very tough and intimidating former military man, attaining the rank of general, and he was also a close friend of William "Butch" Blanchard, commander of the Roswell Army Air Field.

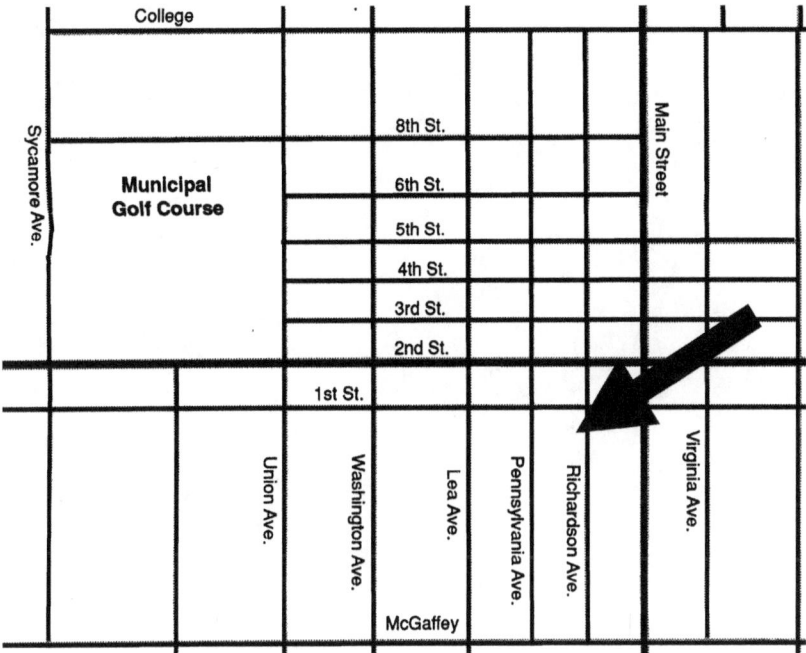

Fire Station near Intersection of 1st St. & Richardson Ave.

Roswell's Fire Station #1, located at 200 South Richardson, was built in 1957 on the very same site as the 1947 Fire Station. When visiting the station, you are standing at the very place where a New Mexico state trooper showed Frankie Rowe and a group of Roswell firefighters pieces of the UFO crash debris, and this is also the place where both an Army colonel and the Roswell City Manager told the firemen never to tell anyone about the crashed

UFO. If you would like to call before visiting the fire station, the number is (575) 624-6700. During your visit, keep in mind that this is an emergency facility, subject to immediate dispatches. Park only in designated areas and remain always aware of emergency vehicles.

FOUR:
ROSWELL POLICE
STATION

Status: Building still standing.
Location: Roswell City Hall, 425 N. Richardson Avenue
Accessibility: City government building.
GPS Coordinates: 33.397388, -104.52432.

Upon arriving at the scene north of town where the UFO actually crashed and bodies were found, Fireman Dan Dwyer noticed a number of Roswell police officers already at the site. "The military had already arrived ... as had some of the city of Roswell police officers. There were also some state police at the site.... It wasn't clear whether they just guarded access to the site or helped clean the field." [Randle & Schmitt, p. 20]

Roswell City Hall, Location of 1947 Police Department

It has also been reported that city police officers were later summoned to assist the military police at the Roswell Army Air Field in securing the area around Building 84, where bodies from the crashed UFO were reportedly taken. The presence of city police outside the hangar has been documented based on eyewitness testimonies compiled by a number of researchers, including Billy Booth of *ufos.about.com*.

In 1993, L. M. Hall, who was a Roswell police officer in 1947, came forward to give an affidavit of his involvement in the strange events of July 1947. Although he was not involved in any of the aforementioned activities at the crash site or at Building 84, he did overhear the local mortician state that the Army had requested several small caskets – the kind used for babies.

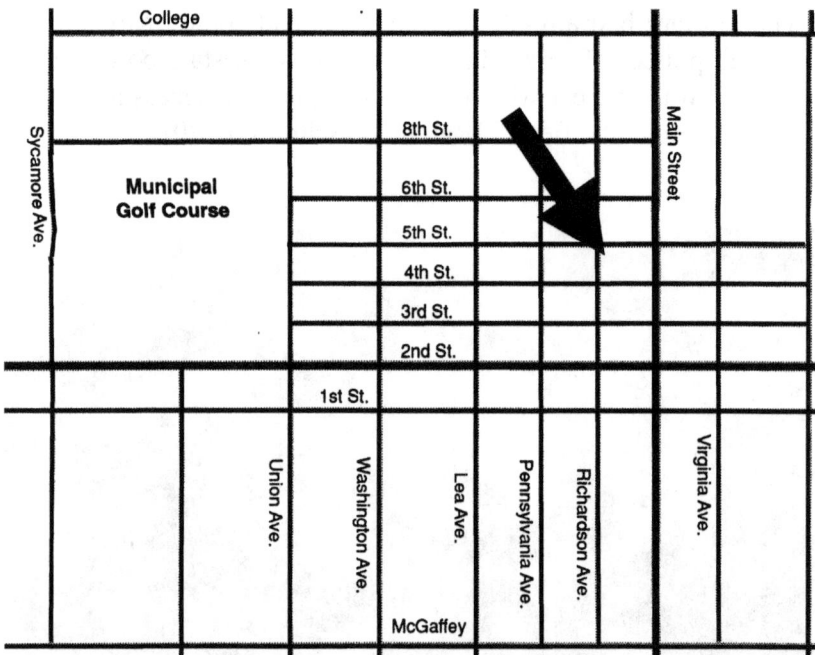

The 1947 Roswell Police Department was housed in what is still City Hall (Near 5th St. & Richardson.)

Hall said in his affidavit, "I came to Roswell, New Mexico, in 1943, while serving in the Army Air Force. I was a military policeman and investigator at Roswell Army Air Field (RAAF). In 1946, after being discharged from the service, I joined the Roswell Police Department, and in 1964 I was appointed chief of police, serving for 14 and a half years. I am now a member of the Roswell City Council.

Another View of Roswell City Hall (Photo by E.J. Wilson)

"In 1947, I was a motorcycle officer, with patrol duty on South Main Street, between town and RAAF. I and other police officers would often take our breaks in the small lounge at the Ballard Funeral Home at 910 South Main, where Glenn Dennis worked. I had gotten to know Glenn when I was a base MP because he made ambulance calls to the base under a contract Ballard's had, so I would sometimes have coffee with him if he was at work when I stopped in.

"One day in July 1947, I was at Ballard's on a break, and Glenn and I were in the driveway 'batting the breeze.' I was sitting on my motorcycle, and Glenn stood nearby. He remarked, 'I had a funny call from the base. They wanted to know if we had several baby caskets.' Then he started laughing and said, 'I asked what for, and they said they wanted to bury [or ship] those aliens,' something to that effect. I thought it was one of those 'gotcha' jokes, so I didn't bite. He never said anything else about it, and I didn't either.

"I believe our conversation took place couple of days after the stories about a crashed flying saucer appeared in the Roswell papers."

According to author Lynn Michelsohn, the Roswell Police Department in 1947 was housed in the building that is still used as City Hall, located at 425 North Richardson Avenue. The building was constructed in 1937 from designs by architect C. R. Carr and partners. As you visit this location, think about the stories of city policemen visiting the Roswell UFO crash site and later helping with security around Building 84. Why did none of them ever come forward and give testimony about their bizarre experience? Perhaps they were kept in the dark by the military as to the exact nature of their assignment on that fateful July in 1947.

FIVE:
SHERIFF'S OFFICE

Status: Demolished in 1996. Stood just east of the courthouse.
Location: 442 North Main Street
Accessibility: Chaves County government property.
GPS Coordinates: 33.397099, -104.521244.

The former Chaves County Sheriff's office and jail, which was built as an annex to the Chaves County Courthouse (on the east side) was demolished in 1996. However, by standing just east of the courthouse, visitors can still be at the very location where Sheriff Wilcox heard ranch Mack Brazel tell his amazing story of finding wreckage from an unidentified flying object.

County Jail and Sheriff's Office in the 1940s
(Courtesy of the Historical Society for Southeast New Mexico)

29

When Brazel came to town after finding the debris at the ranch he stopped by Sheriff Wilcox's office, to see if he might know what the debris was. Not able to identify it, Sheriff Wilcox contacted the military at the RAAF and talked to Intelligence Officer Major Marcel. Some of the debris was hidden at the jail house but later confiscated by the military. However, the most shocking part of the story is what Sheriff Wilcox experienced after Brazel's visit. In a 1995 affidavit, Wilcox's granddaughter, Barbara Dugger, stated, "My grandfather went out there to the [final impact] site; it was in the evening. There was a big burned area, and he saw debris. He also saw four 'space beings.' One of the little men was alive. Their heads were large. They wore suits like silk."

Sheriff George Wilcox (Courtesy of Kevin Randle)

In a 1992 interview with the late Stanton Friedman, Dugger first revealed that the sheriff himself visited the final impact site north of Roswell and saw both wreckage and bodies. Dugger heard the story from her grandmother, Inez Wilcox, the sheriff's wife. Dugger said, "One evening we were watching TV, and on TV was something about space. And my grandmother looked over at me and said, 'Barbara, do you believe in anything, you know, outside the Earth,' and I said, 'You know I do.'" Then, Inez Wilcox told her, "Well, I have something that I'd really like to tell you tonight, but I never want you to discuss it or tell anybody. In the forties, there was a spacecraft, or flying saucer is what she called it, crashed outside of Roswell." When Dugger asked her how she knew, Mrs. Wilcox replied, "Your grandfather George was the sheriff at the time."

East Side of Chaves County Courthouse (Photo by E.J. Wilson)

According to Dugger, Wilcox was never the same after the Roswell Incident. He was shocked by what happened and lived in fear afterward. He expressed no desire to run for re-election as sheriff, and, in fact, Inez Wilcox ran in his place but was defeated. The Wilcox family was indeed deeply scarred by the events of July 1947.

Behind the present-day Chaves County Courthouse stood the L-shaped jailhouse and sheriff's office in 1947. It was here that some of the mysterious debris from the Foster Ranch was kept for a short while. It was also here that Sheriff George Wilcox started a firestorm by contacting the U.S. Army about Mack Brazel's amazing find out at his ranch. It was also here that military police confronted Wilcox and silenced him by threatening both his life and lives of his family members.

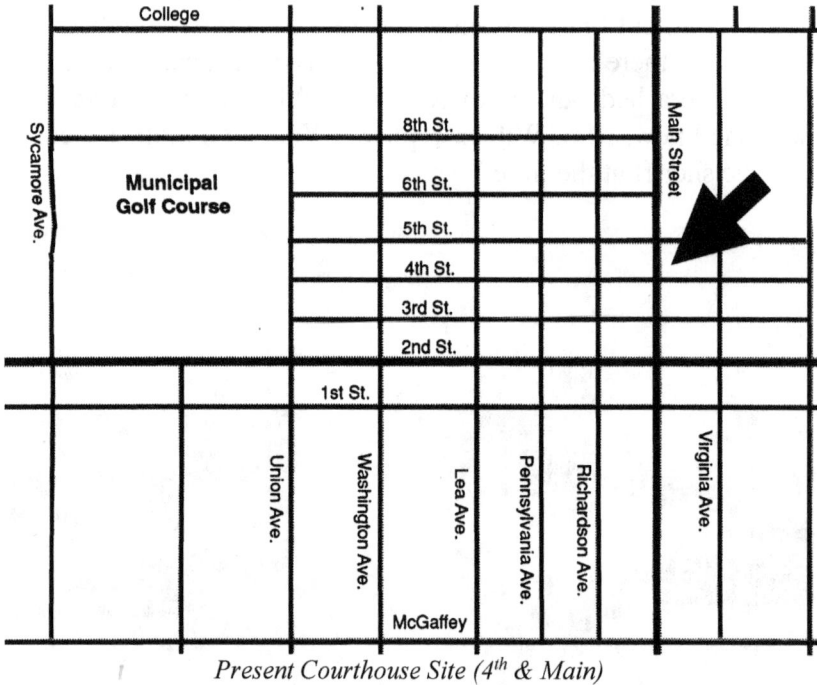

Present Courthouse Site (4th & Main)

Sheriff Wilcox's old office was, unfortunately, demolished in 1996, along with the old jail. However, one can still go and visit the east side of the courthouse and view the location where the building used to be. Standing there in the east parking lot of the courthouse, we can close our eyes and imagine what it must have been like for Sheriff Wilcox when Brazel first came in with his jaw-dropping tale of strange metallic debris that fell out of the sky onto his ranch and the agonizing days and nights Wilcox spent here thinking about what he himself saw out at the crash site.

The east side parking lot is most easily accessed after normal work hours and on weekends. During these times, visitors will not have to contend with the crowds, traffic, and full parking lots that are common during the workday.

SIX:
ROSWELL DAILY
RECORD

Status: Original building demolished in 1997 to clear land for Pioneer Plaza.
Location: 424 North Main Street
Accessibility: City government property. Public access allowed.
GPS Coordinates: 33.397303, -104.522977.

For Americans in the 1940s, newspapers were the last word when it came to the news. Until they saw an item printed in the local newspaper, they did not really believe it. According to the Newspaper Association of America, there were 1,769 daily newspapers in the U.S. in 1947, two of which were published in Roswell, New Mexico – the *Roswell Daily Record* and the *Roswell Morning Dispatch*. Although both papers reported on the UFO crash, the *Daily Record*, which published an evening paper, had the advantage of chance timing when the news broke about a recovered UFO north of town.

Front Page for July 8, 1947 (Wikimedia.org)

Walter G. Haut from 1946 RAAF Yearbook (Courtesy of HSSNM)

On the evening of July 8, the *Daily Record* screamed the headline "RAAF Captures Flying Saucer on Ranch in Roswell Region." The story was based on a press release written by Roswell Army Air Field public information officer Lieutenant Walter Haut. Many years later, Haut stated that the story was an attempt by the military to use the wreckage found at the Foster Ranch as a means to divert attention away from the "second" crash location where the UFO actually went down and bodies were found, some miles away from the Foster Ranch.

The newspaper article stated, "The intelligence office of the 509th Bombardment group at Roswell Army Field announced at noon today, that the field has come into possession of a flying saucer. According to information released by the department, over authority of Maj. J. A. Marcel, intelligence officer, the disk was recovered on a ranch in the Roswell vicinity, after an unidentified rancher had notified Sheriff Geo. Wilcox, here, that he had found the instrument on his premises.

"Major Marcel and a detail from his department went to the ranch and recovered the disk, it was stated. After the intelligence officer here had inspected the instrument it was flown to higher headquarters. The intelligence officer stated that no details of the saucer's construction or its appearance had been revealed."

The article then went on to tell the story of the UFO sighting made by Dan Wilmot and his wife a week earlier. The inclusion of the Wilmot sighting was an apparent attempt by the paper to locate any Roswell residents who might have seen something strange in the skies above town in the same time period.

Pioneer Plaza, Where the Roswell Daily Record Building Once Stood

In a 1993 affidavit, Haut explained what went on behind the scenes prior to the release of the story that later appeared on the front page of the *Roswell Daily Record*. He said, "At approximately 9:30 a.m. on July 8, I received a call from Col. William Blanchard, the base commander, who said he had in his possession a flying saucer or parts thereof. He said it came from a ranch northwest of Roswell, and that the base Intelligence Officer, Major Jesse Marcel, was going to fly the material to Fort Worth." This brief statement by Haut spoke volumes about the logistics of the Roswell crash recovery operation, showing that a plan was already in motion that would slam the lid of secrecy on the whole affair.

"I believe Col. Blanchard saw the material, because he sounded positive about what the material was. There is no chance that he would have mistaken it for a weather balloon. Neither is there any chance that Major Marcel would have been mistaken.... I am convinced that the material recovered was some type of craft from outer space."

Historical Marker Stands near Former Site of the Roswell Daily Record
(Photo by E.J. Wilson)

In 2002, Haut signed another affidavit, which remained sealed until his death in 2005. This second statement gave much more detail about the UFO incident. In it, Haut said, "I was aware that someone had reported the remains of a downed vehicle by mid-morning after my return to duty at the base on Monday, July 7. I was aware that Major Jesse A. Marcel, head of intelligence, was sent by the base commander, Col. William Blanchard, to investigate."

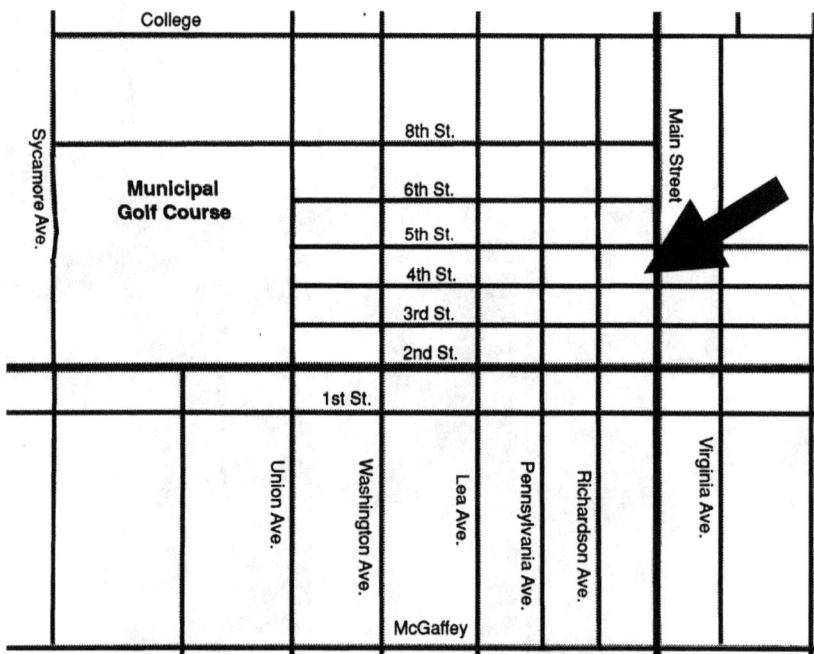

Former Location of the Roswell Daily Record, Near Intersection of Main and 5th

The 2002 affidavit mentions for the first time what UFO investigators had long suspected – that there was a second crash site (other than the Foster Ranch) and that the military was doing everything possible to divert attention from the second crash site by overstating the importance of the debris found at the Foster Ranch. "By late in the afternoon that same day, I would learn that additional civilian reports came in regarding a second site just north of Roswell," Haut said.

At a staff meeting early on July 8, attended by Haut and other Roswell officers, as well as visiting Army officials, it was decided that "attention needed to be diverted from the more important site north of town by acknowledging the other location (Foster Ranch). Too many civilians were already involved, and the press already was informed."

It was then that Colonel Blanchard dictated a press release to Haut, which he was directed to distribute to the two local newspapers and the two local radio stations. The Roswell cover-up was officially underway, researchers claim.

Newspaper Building Was Just Left of This Former Conoco Station
(Photo by E.J. Wilson)

When visiting Pioneer Plaza, where the *Daily Record* building once stood, look to the northern part of the plaza. The newspaper's offices were there at 424 N. Main Street, right next to the former Conoco Service Station, which still stands at 426 N. Main Street. The former service station is now a visitor center.

For the research oriented, all *Roswell Daily Record* newspapers from July 1947 (and many other dates) are available on microfilm at the Roswell Public Library, at 301 N. Pennsylvania

Avenue. Call the library for their hours and additional information, (575) 622-7101, or visit *www.roswellpubliclibrary.org.*

SEVEN:
KGFL RADIO STATION

Status: Building still stands but is now a business, KM Therapeutic Massage.
Location: 310 North Richardson Avenue
Accessibility: Business – open to the public.
GPS Coordinates: 33.395803, -104.524505.

KGFL (*Keep Good Folks Listening*), 1400 AM, was a Roswell radio station that became highly involved in the 1947 UFO incident. The story of small humanoid bodies having been recovered in the Roswell UFO crash first came to light at this historic location. The building that once housed KGFL is now a private business KM Therapeutic Massage, located at the intersection of 3rd Street and North Richardson Avenue.

Radio Station KGFL in the 1940s (Courtesy of HSSNM)

Rancher W.W. "Mack" Brazel in 1947 (Courtesy of HSSNM and the Roswell Daily Record)

On July 6, 1947, KGFL radio announcer Frank Joyce received a phone call from distraught rancher W.W. "Mack" Brazel, who told Joyce an amazing story about strange metallic debris that had rained down upon his ranch and about some foul-smelling bodies that he had discovered. Brazel referred to the bodies as "little people" and told Joyce, "They're not monkeys, and they're not human!"

When Brazel asked Joyce what he should do about the strange things he found on his ranch, Joyce suggested that he contact the Roswell Army Air Field. On the following day, KGFL station owner Walt Whitmore, Sr. arranged to have Brazel brought into town for an exclusive radio interview about his strange find. The interview was conducted on the evening of July 7 at Whitmore's Roswell home, as described in chapter 13.

Meanwhile, on July 8, Roswell Army Air Field Lieutenant Walter Haut stopped by KGFL to deliver the famous "crashed disk" press release, as stated in a 1993 affidavit about the case: "Col. Blanchard told me to write a news release about the operation and to deliver it to both newspapers and the two radio stations in Roswell. He felt that he wanted the local media to have the first opportunity at the story. I went first to KGFL, then to KSWS, then to the Daily Record and finally to the Morning Dispatch."

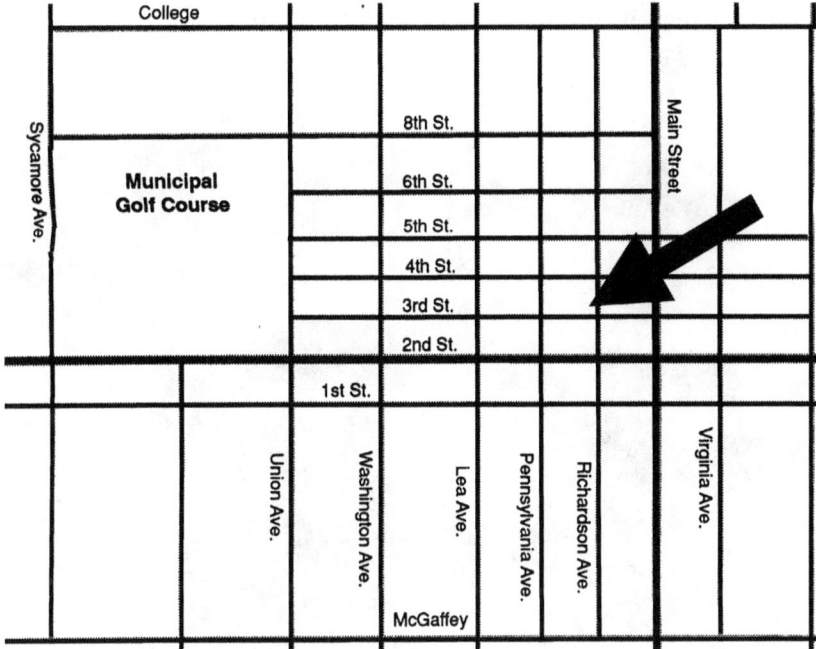

KGFL Site is Near Intersection of 3rd St. & Richardson Ave. (Elegante Hair Salon)

Upon arriving at KGFL, Haut delivered the press release to Frank Joyce. Joyce later told the *Albuquerque Journal*, "He [Haut] comes clumping in and he says, 'Here's your story.' And he's practically going out the door. So I grab the story and I see immediately and it says 'U.S. Army Air Corps has a flying saucer.' And I say, 'Hey, wait a minute. I don't know whether you want to run this.' He said, 'The story is OK.'

"I ran out the door and ran down the block. In 40 seconds, I was to Western Union. I said, 'Send this immediately.' She sent it to Santa Fe, bang, just like that. I waited long enough for her to send it and then grabbed the copy and brought it back with me.

43

Went back to the station. The phone rang and it's Santa Fe bureau, United Press, saying what about this story?

"Then the flash came on, which was five bells. Bing, bing, bing, bing, bing. 'Here it comes,' I said, 'Now all hell is going to break loose.' The phone started ringing. I took the story off the wire and read it (on the air) as a bulletin a couple of times."

Former Site of KGFL Radio Station (Photo by E.J. Wilson)

Some days later, W.W. "Mack" Brazel was brought to KGFL under military escort to revise his earlier story of what he saw out at the Foster Ranch. With the soldiers guarding him standing nearby, Brazel told Joyce that what he saw must have been a weather balloon, as the military insisted. Joyce objected to the substantial changes Brazel was making in his original story and said, "The story is different, especially about the little green men." Brazel responded, almost without thinking, *"They weren't green."* Brazel's statements about seeing strange bodies have become a cornerstone of the Roswell UFO mystery, because previous to the surfacing of these statements, it was believed that Brazel had seen only metallic debris out at his ranch.

When visiting the former KGFL building at 310 North Richardson Avenue, reflect on the important events that took place here. According to Frank Joyce, inside this building Mack Brazel twice referred to finding bodies along with the debris at the Foster Ranch. Brazel described the bodies as being "little" and "not green," and, according to Joyce, he said that they were definitely not humans or monkeys.

EIGHT:
KSWS RADIO STATION

Status: Building still stands. Currently vacant.
Location: 401 N. Richardson Avenue
Accessibility: Private property.
GPS Coordinates: 33.396553, -104.524344.

On July 8, 1947, Lieutenant Walter Haut's second stop while delivering copies of the famous "flying disk" press release was at Roswell AM radio station, KSWS, as he would later testify, "I went first to KGFL, then to KSWS ...."

According to Randle and Schmitt, two days before Haut arrived with the press release, KSWS general manager and part-owner John McBoyle had already been out to the site where the UFO crashed, which he described as being 40 miles north of Roswell, and had seen an object that looked "like a crushed dishpan." McBoyle said the object was 25 to 30 feet long and was impacted into a slope. Stunned by what he saw, McBoyle immediately contacted KOAT, the parent radio station in Albuquerque, New Mexico, to report his discovery.

Typical 1940s Radio Equipment, Displayed at Roswell UFO Museum
(Photo by Noe Torres)

McBoyle's story first came to light in 1993 when an affidavit was filed by Linda Sleppy, who worked at KOAT when the call came in. She said, "In 1947, I worked at KOAT Radio in Albuquerque, New Mexico. My duties included operating the station's teletype machine, which received news and allowed us to send stories to the ABC and Mutual networks, with which KOAT was affiliated.

KSWS is Now a Schlotzky's Deli, Located at 4th & Richardson

She went on to tell of the frantic phone call she received from McBoyle regarding the crash of an unknown object on a ranch north of Roswell. "McBoyle said he had something hot for the network.... Using the teletype, I alerted ABC News headquarters in Hollywood to expect an important story ...."

Sleppy recalled that McBoyle told her, "There's been one of these flying saucer things crash down here north of Roswell." McBoyle added that he had been taking his mid-morning break in a Roswell coffee shop when he saw Mack Brazel come in and tell of finding a strange object while he was out riding on the ranch. Brazel offered to take McBoyle to the ranch to see the object.

Sleppy stated in her affidavit, "As I typed McBoyle's story, a bell rang on the teletype, indicating an interruption. The machine then printed a message something to this effect, '*This is the FBI. You will immediately cease all communication.*' Whatever the precise words were, I definitely remember the message was from the FBI and that it directed me to stop transmitting."

Until 2017, the building that was formerly KSWS was the location of Schlotzky's Deli, at 401 N. Richardson Ave. As of 2019, the building was a Mexican restaurant called *La Gran Victoria*.

Former Location of Radio Station KSWS

NINE:
ROSWELL MORNING
DISPATCH

Status: Still standing. Now the Gift Shop adjacent to UFO Museum.
Location: 114 North Main Street
Accessibility: Business – open to the public.
GPS Coordinates: 33.393563, -104.522909.

The famous press release about the RAAF capturing a flying saucer was delivered to the *Roswell Morning Dispatch* offices by Walter Haut on Tuesday, July 8, 1947. It was the last local media outlet to receive a copy of the report, as Haut had already taken copies to KGFL, KSWS, and the *Roswell Record.*

Front Page from July 9, 1947(Univ. of New Mexico – Albuquerque)

The *Morning Dispatch*, owned by the Dispatch Publishing Company of Roswell, was published daily, except Monday, from October 2, 1928 until March 31, 1950. The newspaper was housed in the small building that is now the gift shop of the *International UFO Museum and Research Center* at 114 North Main Street. It is interesting to note that the *Morning Dispatch* ceased publication less than one year after the Roswell UFO incident, and its operations were absorbed by the *Daily Record*. Is it possible that the newspaper succumbed to pressure over its investigation of the event? Nobody knows for certain. Some UFO researchers have wondered if perhaps the paper attempted to delve more deeply into the Roswell mystery than what the government wanted.

UFO Gift Shop Entrance on Left is the Former Site of Morning Dispatch Newspaper (Photo by E.J. Wilson)

Below is the *Dispatch*'s headline story announcing the crashed UFO, titled "Flying Disk Transforms Sheriff's Office to International Newsroom," from July 9, 1947:

"Reports of the finding of an alleged 'Flying Saucer' approximately 90 miles northwest of here transformed the Chaves county sheriff's office into a full-fledged room of excitement yesterday afternoon as various news agencies from all over the world inquired as to the mysterious object.

"George Wilcox, sheriff, was chained through his desk telephone to newspapers, radio networks, and top officials on an

international scope as the long-distance wires buzzed with continuous requests for his office.

"The furor started Monday when W. W. Brazel, a rancher living on the old Foster place, 25 miles southeast of Corona, New
Mexico, came in the office and reported finding an object which
fitted the descriptions of the flying discs. Deputy Sheriff B. A.
Clark, who handled the report, immediately notified Sheriff Wilcox, who in turn turned his information over to Army authorities
at RAAF.

"According to Mr. Brazel, the object had the shape of a box
kite. It was broken in two. The size of the alleged disc was, contrary to previous descriptions, rectangular, and measured
approximately three feet by four feet.

"Major Jesse A. Marcel of the 509th Bomb Group Intelligence
and an Army crew immediately went to the ranch and picked up
the object. No member of the local sheriff's office saw the article
at any time. Army sources did not divulge any description either
of the outside or internal appearance of the disc.

"Following the news release of the report, Sheriff Wilcox was
the object of a storm of inquiries from papers in San Francisco,
Boston, Los Angeles, New York, New Orleans, Baltimore, St.
Louis, Denver, Albuquerque, Milwaukee, Santa Fe, Chicago,
Washington, and Mexico City. The longest call came from London, England where the London Daily Mail and other newspapers
desired information.

"The major radio networks, including N.B.C., C.B.S., Trans
Radio, plus the Associated and United Press and International
News Service also contacted Wilcox. Others in the cavalcade
were Paramount News and International News Photo.

"The stream of calls continued to such an extent that the plac-
ing of outgoing messages was almost impossible. If by chance
the phone ceased ringing for time enough to pick it up, the operator would immediately ask whether or not it was the sheriff's
office, and then state that there was another long-distance call
coming through.

"The London operator, with the very pronounced 'H's' and
the 'rather' presented a translation problem to the sheriff, and the

strong contrast between the Western drawl and the English twang was both interesting and amusing. In response to various queries, Sheriff Wilcox could only state the location of the spot where the object was found and the name of the person finding it. Any descriptions other than its reported size were not available."

The managing editor of the *Morning Dispatch* in 1947 was Arthur R. McQuiddy, who later gave a sworn affidavit regarding what he knew about the Roswell UFO crash: "In July 1947, I was editor of the *Roswell Morning Dispatch*, one of the two newspapers here at the time. In 1948, I left the paper to become public relations director of the New Mexico Oil and Gas Association and later joined U.S. Steel as director of media relations. About eleven years ago I returned to Roswell after retiring as senior vice president for corporate relations at International Harvester.

"Just before noon one day early in July 1947, Walter Haut, the public relations officer at Roswell Army Air Field (RAAF), brought a press release to me in the Dispatch office. The release said a crashed flying saucer had been found, taken to RAAF, and sent on to another base.

"Haut had been to the two local radio stations, KGFL and KSWS, before coming to the *Dispatch*, so I gave him a bad time about that. Haut said the base policy was to rotate who got releases first to make sure everyone got a fair shake. We were a morning paper, so our edition for that day had long since hit the street, but I was disappointed at not being able to break the story on the Associated Press wire. George Walsh, the program manager at KSWS, had already moved the story on AP.

"Not long after Haut left, a call came from RAAF. The caller said the release was incorrect, that what had been thought to be the wreckage of a flying saucer were actually the remains of a radiosonde balloon. However, the AP wire story had gotten the world's attention. I spent the rest of the afternoon taking long distance calls from overseas news editors. I remember calls from Rome, London, Paris, and Hong Kong.

"Colonel William H. ('Butch') Blanchard, commander of RAAF and its 509th Bomb Group, was a good friend of mine. We often got together for a drink and off the record discussions of base-town relations and the like. After the flying saucer incident, I tried several times to get Blanchard to tell me the real story, but he repeatedly refused to talk about it.

"About three or four months after the event, when we were a bit more 'relaxed' than usual, I tried again. Blanchard reluctantly admitted he had authorized the press release. Then, as best I remember, he said, 'I will tell you this and nothing more. The stuff I saw, I've never seen anyplace else in my life.' That was all he would say, and he never told me anything else about the matter."

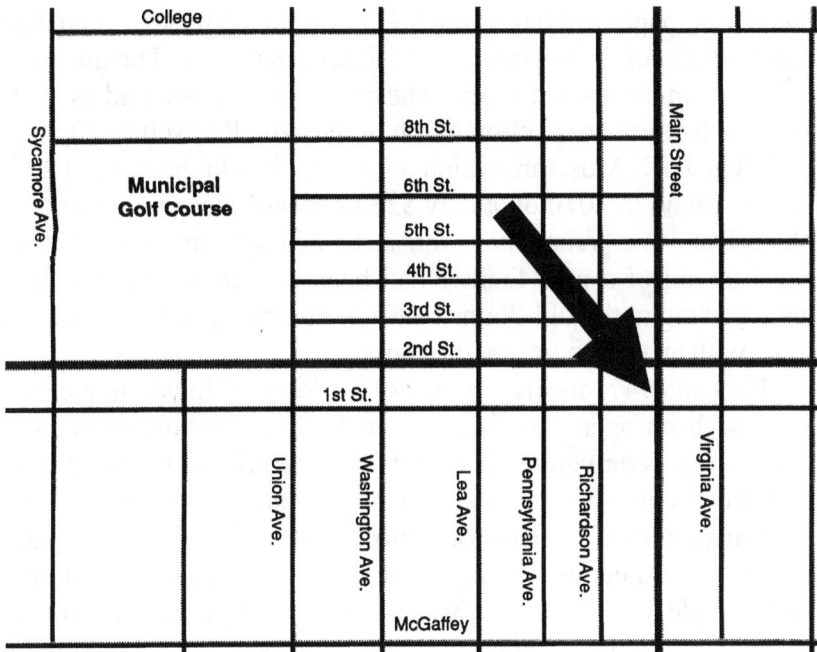

The Morning Dispatch Building is now the UFO Museum Gift Shop at 1st & Main

TEN:
PLAINS THEATER / UFO
MUSEUM

Status: Still standing and is now the Roswell UFO Museum.
Location: 114 North Main Street
Accessibility: Business – open to the public (admission).
GPS Coordinates: 33.39369, -104.522903.

Next door to the former offices of the *Roswell Morning Dispatch* newspaper is the Roswell UFO Museum, whose official title is *International UFO Museum and Research Center*. The museum is housed in the former Plains Theater, built in 1946, and as such shares a historic connection to the time of the Roswell UFO incident. The UFO Museum, which opened in the old theater in 1997, broke ground in 2010 on a new $25 million-dollar museum complex. But, one year later, museum officials announced that construction of a new facility had been cancelled and that they were staying at the old Plains Theater, having signed a long-term lease with an option to buy the property.

Back in 1947, during the time of the Roswell Incident, the theater had been open less than a year. Designed by architect Jack Corgan for a company called Theater Enterprises, it was built of reinforced concrete and featured 1,000 seats on the main floor with an additional 30 seats for "colored patrons" located off to one side of the projection booth. The theater was done in an "art moderne" style and its exterior was adorned with an elegant vertical sign and a triangle marquee. Theater patrons in 1947 would have included servicemen stationed at the Roswell Army Air Field. Not only were the soldiers frequent patrons at Roswell's six movie houses, but they occasionally even worked part-time there during the evening hours.

In July 1947, of Roswell's six indoor movie theaters, the Plains Theater was easily the newest and most popular of them all. The others were: the Yucca, the Chief, the Trieb, the Chavez, and the Pecos.

1947 Photo of the Plains Theater (Courtesy of HSSNM)

During the week ending July 9, the Plains Theater was show-ing the Western "Cheyenne," starring Dennis Morgan and Jane Wyman. Morgan played a gambler who agreed to try to catch a mysterious stage coach robber known only as "The Poet." No Hollywood plot, however, could come close to the shocking events that were about to unfold in the quiet town of Roswell. In a story beyond belief, the reported crash of a UFO north of town was about to set off a ripple effect that would continue for decades to come.

And so, eventually, the Plains Theater became the Interna-tional UFO Museum and Research Center. Founded as a non-profit organization in 1991 by two men deeply involved in the Roswell Incident, Walter Haut and Glenn Dennis, the museum opened to the public in 1992. It was housed at two different down-town locations before moving to the old Plains Theater in 1997.

The museum was an immediate success and now receives about 150,000 visitors per year. It was named "Top Tourist Destination of New Mexico" by the Tourism Association of New Mexico in 1996 and also "New Mexico's "Main Street Business of the Year" in 2003. Another high honor came in 2003, when Roswell, including its famous museum, was listed in Patricia Schultz's bestselling book, *1,000 Places to See Before You Die.*

Roswell UFO Museum (Photo by E.J. Wilson)

In 1995, the museum held Roswell's very first UFO Festival during the first week of July in commemoration of the July 1947 Roswell Incident. The festival was another smashing success for the museum, and two years later, 50,000 people showed up for the 1997 festival. Suddenly, Roswell residents, many of who were uninformed or apathetic about the famous UFO incident, began viewing the annual festival as a win-win situation for the city.

Recognizing opportunities to revitalize the town's sagging economy, local officials locked on to the suddenly-explosive "UFO tourism" business. Hoping to capitalize on the museum's success, the city began supplementing the museum festival events with city-sponsored special events throughout Roswell.

UFO Researcher Ruben Uriarte (middle) with Two Friends at the Roswell Museum's 2010 UFO Festival (Courtesy of Ruben Uriarte)

In 2011, according to Roswell television station KOB, an economic study revealed that the UFO Museum "brings in an estimated $57 million into the state's economy and attracts around 150,000 visitors each year."

The *International UFO Museum and Research Center* is typically open every day of the year from 9 a.m. to 5 p.m. For exact information on hours and admission fees, please contact the museum on its worldwide toll-free phone number, 1-800-822-3545. The museum's Roswell telephone number is (575) 625-9495. A self-guided audio tour is available – just ask at the front desk.

The main floor of the museum features a large area of exhibits related to the Roswell Incident, and consisting of photographs, newspaper clippings, artifacts, dioramas, models, and other items. One of the most eye-catching exhibits is a recreation of the "alien autopsy" scene from *Roswell*, the 1994 *Showtime* original motion picture produced by Paul Davids. The exhibit contains actual props from the movie, including an extremely realistic-looking dead alien being.

"Alien Autopsy" Exhibit at the UFO Museum in Roswell
(Photo by Ruben Uriarte)

Other exhibits focus on the UFO phenomenon in general, with displays on topics such as crop circles, Area 51, interstellar travel, the Lubbock Lights, and so on. For museum visitors to fully benefit from their visit, they will need time to slowly wind around the museum and spend a lot of time reading textual matter in the displays. Given the museum's steadfast thesis that UFOs are real, its exhibits are research-oriented and content-rich, rather than being strictly "visual" or entertainment-oriented. Since lot of reading, thinking, and digesting of information is required, you should allow at least two hours, and possibly four, to fully appreciate this incredible storehouse of UFO information.

Stanton Friedman (left) and Noe Torres (right) at the Roswell UFO Museum's 2010 Festival (Photo by Ruben Uriarte)

Balloons Above the Museum Mark the Start of the Roswell UFO Festival

In addition to the wealth of exhibits on the main floor, the museum also boasts a large library featuring an extensive collection of UFO-related books and other materials. The library is a boon to everyone wanting to delve further into the Roswell Incident or into almost any topic related to UFOs and the paranormal.

Opening Ceremony for Roswell Museum's UFO Festival in 2010
(Photo by Ruben Uriarte)

Exploration of the UFO museum is an absolute necessity for everyone following the touring plan in this book. We recommend visiting the museum as your last stop, after having visited all the key locations related to the Roswell Incident. Plan to spend at least four hours browsing the displays. Although we recommend visiting the museum last, some readers may prefer to "do their homework" first, in preparation for their touring – and this is certainly fine, too.

ELEVEN:
MILITARY CONVOY
ROUTE

Status: Public road.
Location: Hwy 285 (S. Main St.) from north to south, through town.
Accessibility: Public roadway.
GPS Coordinates – Start (2nd & Main): 33.39424, -104.522772.
End (Former Roswell Army Air Field): 33.314947, -104.523301.

As you head south toward the old air base to continue your tour of the key Roswell sites, you will be retracing the route taken by a very strange military convoy that reportedly moved through town back in July 1947. According to a number of eyewitnesses, after the crashed UFO was recovered north of town by the military, it was put on a truck, covered with a tarp, and paraded right down the middle of town in broad daylight.

From its crash location somewhere north of Roswell, the downed UFO was reportedly hoisted onto a U.S. Army flatbed trailer (called a "lowboy"), covered almost completely by a tarp, and then pulled by a tractor truck south on U.S. Highway 285, through the middle of Roswell. A number of jeeps carrying soldiers armed with machine guns accompanied the truck as it made its way through the town in broad daylight and on to Building 84 at the Roswell Army Air Field.

Though the strange object was covered by a tarp, some townspeople who watched the convoy pass by described the shape underneath the tarp as egg-shaped or conical, according to Carey and Schmitt. Another witness said the shape under the tarp looked like a Volkswagen Beetle. Yet another witness, who was in the middle of a roofing job as the convoy passed, claimed to have seen pieces of mangled metal on the flatbed trailer as well.

As you move south on Main Street, headed to the next touring sites, think about what it must have been like to witness that military convoy, carrying with it the strange tarp-covered object that some people say was a crashed UFO. It was most certainly an awe-inspiring site, especially since most of Roswell's residents had already heard rumors that something very strange had crashed north of town and that the military was involved in retrieving the downed airship. Although it may seem strange that the military would choose to transport the UFO through the middle of town during daylight hours, researchers say that their options were very limited.

Roswell's Main Street in the 1940s (Courtesy of HSSNM)

Why would the military take the risk of moving the alien craft in plain view of the entire town? The reason was probably alarm over how many civilians had already heard of the top-secret recovery operation. Already a significant number of private citizens had found out about the second crash location, where the main part of the craft and bodies had come down. Also, rumors of a crashed UFO were sweeping through town, putting pressure on the Army to act rapidly and decisively.

Convoy Path through Town and On to Bldg. 84

Given that military convoys were not an uncommon sight in Roswell, the decision was made to proceed with the transport by the quickest and most efficient route – straight through town. It was a dramatic and daring gamble, and yet, for the most part, it worked. Very few Roswell citizens took much notice of the strange early morning military procession down Main Street. Hiding the UFO "in plain sight," ended up being a successful strategy for the U.S. Army.

Interestingly, every Fourth of July, the city of Roswell holds a UFO parade down Main Street, starting at College Boulevard and heading south on Main. Floats and dioramas depict various scenes involving crashed saucers and "cute" looking aliens. While watching the odd assemblage of vehicles and floats pass by, one cannot help but find a strange irony in the fact that this was the actual route that was reportedly taken by the U.S. Army in 1947 when transporting the crashed UFO to the Roswell Army Air Field.

This scenario reminds one of the so-called "cargo" cults of the South Pacific, where isolated islanders saw U.S. airplanes flying overhead during World War II. Because they had never before seen aircraft, they proceeded to build mock planes and incorporate them into their religious festivals. They built faux runways, control towers, planes, and electronic equipment in honor of the amazing flying machines and associated instruments that they saw the U.S. servicemen using. Is it possible that, confronted with technology that is light years beyond ours, Americans reacted in a manner similar to these cargo cults?

TWELVE:
BALLARD FUNERAL
HOME

Status: Still standing.
Location: 910 South Main Street
Accessibility: Business (funeral home).
GPS Coordinates: 33.383979, -104.522999.

On a hot afternoon in July 1947, 22-year-old Glenn Dennis was working as an embalmer at the Ballard Funeral Home, which held a contract to provide mortuary services and ambulance services for the Roswell Army Air Field, when the phone suddenly rang, and he answered. In a 1991 affidavit, Dennis recalled, "One afternoon, around 1:15 or 1:30, I received a call from the base mortuary officer who asked what was the smallest size hermetically sealed casket that we had in stock. He said, 'We need to know this in case something comes up in the future.' He asked how long it would take to get one, and I assured him I could get one for him the following day. He said he would call back if they needed one."

Glenn Dennis

Although the call seemed very strange, Dennis put it out of his mind and returned to his work at the funeral home. Within an hour, the phone rang again, and the same Army mortuary officer asked Dennis "to describe the preparation for bodies that had been lying out on the desert for a period of time." Dennis said.

Another View of Ballard Funeral Home (Photo by E.J. Wilson)

"Before I could answer, he said he specifically wanted to know what effect the preparation procedures would have on the body's chemical compounds, blood and tissues. I explained that our chemicals were mainly strong solutions of formaldehyde and water, and that the procedure would probably alter the body's chemical composition. I offered to come out to the base to assist with any problem he might have, but he reiterated that the information was for future use. I suggested that if he had such a situation that I would try to freeze the body in dry ice for storage and transportation."

Once again, the call ended and Dennis returned to his work, still puzzled by the strange requests from the air base. A little over an hour later, yet another call came in to him from the base. This time, the military requested that Dennis pick up a soldier that had been injured in a motorcycle accident in town. As instructed, Dennis took the injured soldier south of town to the Roswell Army

Air Field hospital building. Upon arrival, he assisted the young man out of the ambulance and was helping him up the ramp toward the rear entrance of the hospital, when he became aware of strange activity going on there.

Glenn Dennis (Courtesy of Kevin D. Randle)

Ballard Funeral Home (Photo by E.J. Wilson)

As Dennis passed a military ambulance with its back door open, he noticed that it contained a metallic structure shaped like the bottom of a canoe and containing strange writing or symbols on it, like hieroglyphics. As we will see in a later chapter, nothing could have prepared Dennis for what he was to discover next, upon stepping into the RAAF hospital building.

The Ballard Funeral Home is still in business at the same location, 910 South Main Street, as in 1947. When stopping by to look over the building, visitors are asked to be considerate of funeral services that may be ongoing there.

Located at Intersection of S. Main & Summit St. (BLM Map)

THIRTEEN:
WHITMORE RESIDENCE

Status: Residence still stands.
Location: 204 W. McGaffey Street
Accessibility: Private residence.
GPS Coordinates: 33.379688, -104.525562.

On July 7, 1947, after KGFL radio announcer Frank Joyce talked by phone with rancher Mack Brazel, who claimed to have found wreckage and bodies at his ranch, radio station owner Walt Whitmore, Sr. became entranced by the story. Realizing that Brazel's tale had the potential to become a world-wide news sensation, Whitmore began formulating a plan to obtain an exclusive radio interview with the rancher.

Former Residence of Walt Whitmore, Sr. (Photo by E.J. Wilson)

Depending on the version of the story, Whitmore either drove out to the Foster Ranch or sent someone in his place, to pick up Brazel. Either way, Brazel was persuaded to come into Roswell, spend the night at Whitmore's house, and be interviewed for radio.

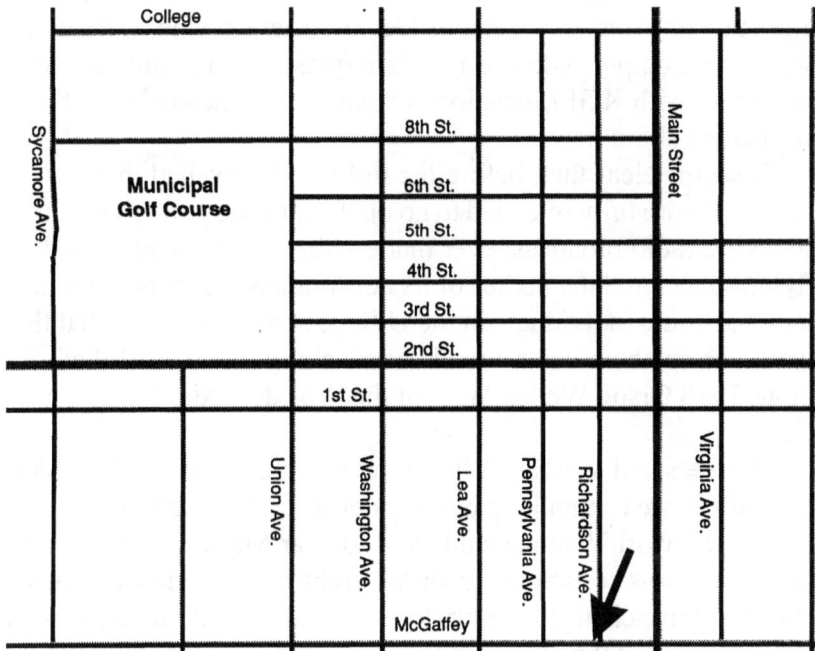

Former Whitmore Residence, Near Intersection of Richardson Ave & McGaffey

According to *Witness to Roswell* by Carey and Schmitt, KGFL newsman George "Jud" Roberts, recorded the interview with Brazel late on the evening of July 7 at Whitmore's home in Roswell. By all accounts, it was an interview that would blow the lid of secrecy off the entire affair, and KGFL fully intended to broadcast it – but not until the following day. Because the station was already off the air by the time the interview was taped, the radio station personnel planned to broadcast it the next day, July 8. Unfortunately, early the next morning, the military showed up, took Brazel away to temporary confinement at the Roswell Army Air

Field, and also confiscated the recordings made by Roberts on the previous evening.

In addition, Roberts received a phone call from an official of the Federal Communications Commission stating that if KGFL aired anything about the Brazel interview, the station would lose its license to broadcast. This call was followed moments later by a phone call from U.S. senator Dennis Chavez, who advised the station to comply with the FCC's request. As a result, Brazel's interview with KGFL was lost, except in the memories of those who knew about it.

It seems clear that, before the military intervened in the matter, Whitmore fully intended to go on the air with perhaps the most shocking radio broadcast ever made – the discovery of a crashed flying saucer and the bodies of its non-human occupants. It is certain that some individuals in the U.S. government feared that this would bring about a nationwide panic along the lines of the infamous 1938 Orson Welles "War of the Worlds" radio broadcast by CBS.

As we stand viewing Whitmore's former home at 204 West McGaffey, we cannot help but wonder what the result might have been if the world had been allowed to hear Mack Brazel's amazing eyewitness testimony recorded right here inside this house. Would it have changed the world, or would the military have been able to discredit it as they did the Foster Ranch debris?

The house where Whitmore once lived is a private residence, and visitors are cautioned not to trespass or disturb its current occupants. Use caution and common sense when taking pictures of the home and surrounding area.

FOURTEEN:
ST. MARY'S HOSPITAL

Status: Demolished. Site is now Chaves County Administration Building
Location: 1 St. Mary's Place
Accessibility: Chaves County government building.
GPS Coordinates: 33.375987, -104.521726.

On the evening of July 4 between 11:00 and 11:30 p.m., a log entry was made by two Franciscan Catholic nuns observing the night sky atop St. Mary's Hospital in Roswell. Mother Superior Mary Bernadette and Sister Capistrano reported seeing a flaming object falling toward Earth at a point north of their position. They speculated that it was an airplane in distress. This prompted them to record the incident in their nightly log, but they made no further inquiry into the strange sighting, and it was many years later before their log entry was discovered.

St. Mary's Hospital in the Early 1960s (Courtesy of HSSNM)

Chaves County Administrative Center, on Former Site of St. Mary's Hospital (Photo by E.J. Wilson)

The nuns' sighting was recently summarized on the *tinwiki.org* Web site as follows: "Two Catholic nuns, reported to be Mother Superior Mary Bernadette and a Sister Capistrano, report seeing a bright fiery object appear to go to the ground well to the west and slightly north of Roswell, possibly in the mountains or beyond, late in the evening while looking out a third floor window of the now demolished Saint Mary's Hospital during the change of their shift, recording its passage in their logbook. They make no mention of an explosion, perhaps because of the distance the object went down from where they were, although some reports say the nuns saw a large flash in the night sky in the exact place on the horizon at the same time they lost eye contact with the object."

St. Mary's Hospital was the city's first medical facility, having been established in 1906 by nuns of the Roman Catholic nursing order, Sisters of the Sorrowful Mother. It was the birthplace of a number of celebrities, including singer John Denver and motion picture actress Demi Moore.

The hospital was purchased by Chaves County in 1989 and became part of Eastern New Mexico Medical Center, which the county had operated since 1955. The aging St. Mary facility was finally demolished in 1999, and on the lot where it once stood, the county built the green-domed Chaves County Administration Offices, also called the Joseph R. Skeen Building.

Arrow Shows Former Location of St. Mary's Hospital (BLM Map)

The new building is located at 1 St. Mary's Place and is a public facility that is open to visitors during regular business hours. You are asked to park only in designated visitor parking spaces, and be careful not to interfere with any of the county operations going on at the facility. You may also choose to visit outside of the normal business hours in order to encounter less hectic conditions. After hours, you will not be able to enter the building, but you can walk around outside, take pictures, and look to the northwest, where the nuns claimed to have seen the fiery object crash to the earth in July 1947. Their account of seeing a flying vehicle in the skies above town prior to the reported UFO crash is a very significant moment in the history of the Roswell Incident.

FIFTEEN:
RAAF CHAPEL

Status: Public house of worship.
Current Location: 206 East Charleston Road, just off of South Main Street.
Original Location: N.W. of the intersection of University Blvd. & Mathis St.
Accessibility: Church open to the public during hours when services are held.
GPS Coordinates: 33.335952, -104.519354.

A church building is normally thought of as a place of refuge during times of both spiritual and actual danger. In July 1947, the small chapel at the Roswell Army Air Field was, without a doubt, at the center of a swirling firestorm of intense emotions and extreme tensions. Talk was "in the air" about a strange UFO crash site north of town. Eyewitnesses spoke in hushed tones about small bodies that were not human and pieces of debris that nobody on Earth could have made.

The Former RAAF Chapel (Photo by E.J. Wilson)

Although the former RAAF chapel still exists today, it has been moved from its original location on the air base and can now be found about two miles north of where it was in 1947. Back then, according to Roswell historian Elvis Fleming, the white, wood frame chapel stood with its lonely steeple rising into the sky in what is now an empty lot at the northwest corner of the inter-section of University Boulevard and Mathis Street. "That chapel originally was across the street just west of the present Arts and Sciences Center. When I came to Eastern New Mexico University at Roswell in 1969, I was told that it had been the Catholic chapel.... It was all boarded up and was being used for storage when I arrived on the scene," Fleming remembers.

Map Shows Location of Former RAAF Catholic Chapel

In their book *Witness to Roswell*, Carey and Schmitt discuss reports that some of the RAAF personnel had difficulty coping with what they saw and experienced in July 1947. Some turned to

alcohol; others became suicidal. Suddenly and dramatically realizing that they had been visited by beings from beyond the Earth,
some of the soldiers most certainly sought out the quiet solitude
of the RAAF chapel to reflect on the end of their innocent view of
the universe. Jesse Marcel, Jr., who was 11 years old at the time,
later wrote, "The experience as definitely a 'game changer' in my
life…. Suddenly and profoundly, I realized that human beings are
not alone in the vast cosmos and that God's unbounded creative
energies did not begin or end with the creation of life on Earth."

Another View of the Former RAAF Chapel (Photo by E.J. Wilson)

At the time of the Roswell UFO crash, according to Carey
and Schmitt, services at the RAAF chapel were conducted by a
Protestant minister, the Reverend Elijah H. Hankerson of the Na-
tional Baptist Convention. Then abruptly, on July 10, 1947 – in
the midst of the Roswell Incident – the Army suddenly, on very
short notice, transferred Hankerson and brought in Captain William B. Benson, a Roman Catholic priest. The sudden switch has
led to speculation that the Army was stepping up its "damage control" in the wake of the continuing Roswell crisis. Perhaps the

Army leaders felt better having a member of the Catholic priesthood, steeped in its long tradition of dealing with deep spiritual crises in a confidential manner.

According to researcher Anthony Bragalia, the displaced Reverend Hankerson never mentioned having been stationed in Roswell, even to relatives. Family members say that, later in life, Hankerson, who died in 1990, seemed haunted by something from his past that had changed his perspective on life and on the universe. He was often heard repeating, as if in a trance, several phrases, including, "The universe is amazing," and "I am just a man."

In the 1970s, the former RAAF chapel was moved to its present location at 206 East Charleston Road, not far from the old air base. As of this writing, it is listed as the meeting place for the Mountain View Baptist Church, a member of the Reformed or Sovereign Grace Churches of New Mexico. For more information about the church and its schedule of services, please visit their web site at *http://mtviewbaptistchurch.com*.

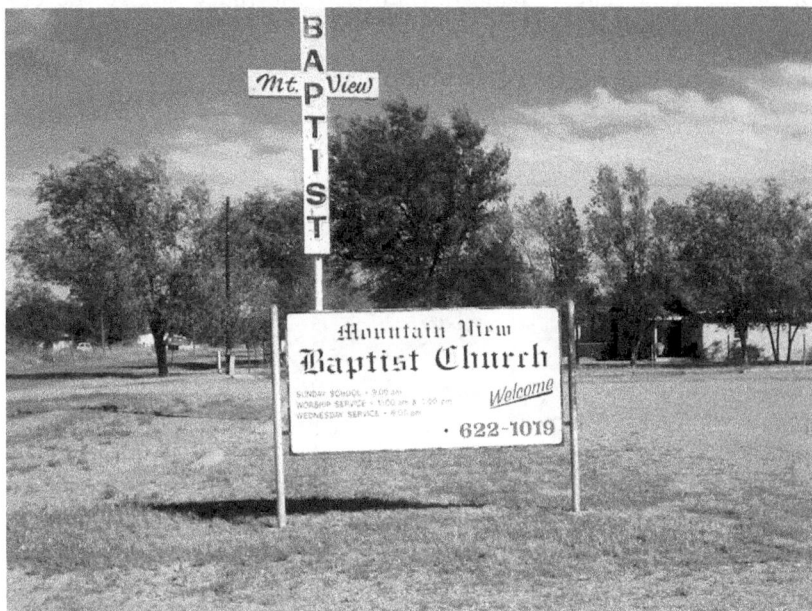

Sign for Mountain View Baptist Church (Photo by E.J. Wilson)

SIXTEEN: RAAF ENTRANCE / MAIN GATE

Status: Entrance no longer restricted. Guard house no longer in place.
Location: Slightly north of intersection of S. Main St. & W. Byrne St.
Accessibility: Public roadway.
GPS Coordinates: 33.320842, -104.523561.

Roswell Army Air Field, like all military bases, had a guard house at its main gate, and everyone entering or exiting the base was scrutinized by the military police on duty. The guard house, which was removed after the air base was decommissioned in 1967, stood just northwest of the intersection of South Main Street and West Byrne Street. Today, there is no trace of the guard house or pillars, but visitors can walk around the place where the entrance to the base used to be.

1960s Photo of Roswell Air Base Main Gate (Courtesy of Clifford Bossie)

There are two interesting stories associated with the main gate of the Roswell Army Air Field. First, when the Army reportedly brought the crashed UFO on a flatbed trailer through the town of Roswell, the convoy, consisting of the truck-trailer and its jeep escort, pulled through the main gate of the base, right here past the guard house, and continued south along Walker Boulevard.

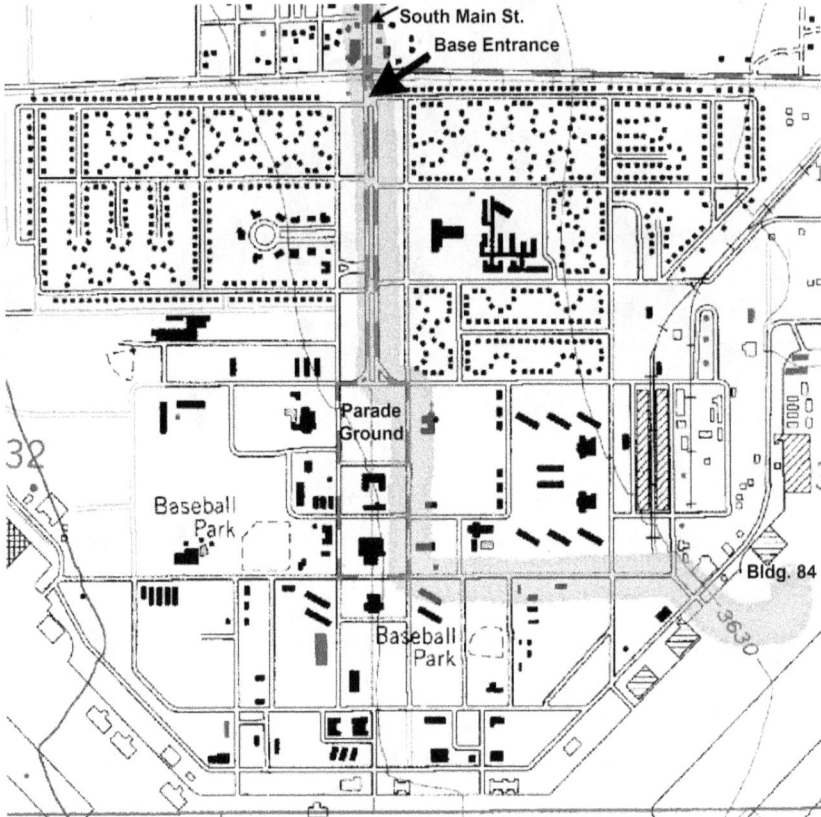

Map Shows Convoy Route to Bldg. 84 (USGS Map)

After passing here, the convoy turned east onto what is now East Martin Street and then south along present-day Gail Harris Street, and finally east on East Mathis Street, to Building 84. Once there, the top-secret materials on the flatbed trailer were unloaded into Building 84, which was the base's most secure aircraft hangar. As the story goes, several witnesses later saw an airship of unknown design inside Building 84, as well as some "non-human" bodies. There were also reports that one of the small creatures recovered at the UFO crash site was still alive when it was brought to Building 84.

Current Entrance to the Roswell Air Center (Photo by E.J. Wilson)

In his book *Roswell USA: Towns That Celebrate UFOs, Lake Monsters, Bigfoot, and Other Weirdness*, Roswell historian John LeMay tells the amazing story of the alien that was reportedly shot by guards at the front entrance to the base. LeMay writes:

> In 1997, while giving tours of his ranch, believed by some to have been the final impact site, farmer Hub Corn said that three dead aliens were recovered from his ranch and a 'live' one was found sitting "on that rock over yonder." Corn also said the alien was holding onto a small black box and when the military showed up, they had to hit him on the head with a rifle butt to get him to let go of it.
>
> The account first brought to light in John Tilley's *Expose: Roswell UFO Incident* of a live alien being shot by

the military is one of the more interesting theories regarding what possibly happened to the alleged survivor of the crash.

In the story as related to Tilley by Hieck, the alien escaped the base somehow and made its way outside the base gate to a cluster of small houses that were occupied mainly by base personnel and their families. "There were small apartments, and a trailer court, and a store, and a dry cleaners, and things like that, and [the alien] was peering through windows…and scaring the heck out of people like I wrote in my book," Tilley said. After its adventurous wanderings amidst the local residences, the creature made its way back to the RAAF main entrance gate, where startled guards shot first and asked questions later.

Also supporting the notion that a crash survivor was later killed by military are the oft-debated, cryptic remarks of a photographer, who was supposedly called in by the military to take pictures of the aftermath of the crash. The photographer, whose name will not be used at the request of his family, rarely spoke about his role in the incident, except to utter the vague statement, "They killed it." The context of the statement has never been clarified. Some believe he was referring to the Roswell story itself being silenced, and therefore "killed," by the government, while others think he was referring to one of the aliens having been killed.

UFO investigator Jim Marrs believed the statement was about a dead alien, based on his conversation with a close relative of the photographer. When Marrs asked the family member if "they killed it" meant that the story had been squelched, the response was a smile and the statement: "No, I think he meant they killed one of them.'"

When I asked another family member about the photographer's alleged comments, he said with some consternation that he is often misquoted by researchers and didn't know much more about the story.

Some who hear this account for the first time are bothered not by the fact that a living alien had been recovered at the crash site, but rather by the idea that it somehow slipped away from military confinement, which is something that even Mack Brazel couldn't accomplish. John Tilley also finds this puzzling. "I have no idea how that thing would have gotten away from 'em. The room had to have been guarded or should have had MPs all around that place, but it got away from them, according to the story, and made its way off base," Tilley said. One would expect that the crash survivor would have been more closely guarded, but then again, massive confusion dominated the base following the incident, as noted by several witnesses, including Glenn Dennis. Perhaps the survivor's guards were momentarily distracted in the chaos sweeping through the base. Perhaps the alien had skills or abilities unknown to us that facilitated its escape.

Another theory is that the alien was at first believed to be dead but was actually only unconscious or in some form of suspended animation or trance. It may have been grouped with the bodies of the others, only to awaken later and find itself unguarded. Taking advantage of the prevailing confusion on the base, it got up and quietly slipped away on foot. All of this is, of course, sheer speculation.

As pointed out by LeMay, the alien is said to have gotten away from its guards by unknown means and was later seen peeking through the windows of several homes located in a trailer park just northwest of the base's main gate. The apparition certainly must have terrified the local residents, and the reaction of the humans probably, in turn, also frightened the creature.

The guards at the base entrance saw the alien coming out of the trailer park area, and supposedly, they panicked, fired upon it, and inadvertently killed it. Although this story remains unverified and is considered a legend, it remains, to this day, one of the more interesting bits of lore revolving around the 1947 Roswell Incident.

An alien cut out now greets visitors to Town and Country Mobile Home and R.V. Park near the old air base in Roswell. (Photo by John LeMay)

SEVENTEEN:
RAAF GUEST HOUSE

Status: Empty lot – building gone.
Location: Intersection of West Byrne St. & South Main St.
Accessibility: Private property.
GPS Coordinates: 33.321056, -104.5238.

Immediately adjacent to where the RAAF entrance and guard house once stood, there was a small wooden building that in 1947 was known as the RAAF "guest house." In this building, rancher W.W. "Mack" Brazel was held by the military for five days, and during this time, the Army apparently persuaded him to change his story about the debris he found on his ranch.

The Former RAAF Guest House, North Side (Photo by E.J. Wilson)

Brazel was brought to the guest house after spending the evening of July 7, 1947 at the home of KGFL radio station owner Walt Whitmore, Sr., during which he was interviewed on tape about the mysterious debris he found at the Foster Ranch. During the interview, which was never aired, he reportedly also mentioned having seen the bodies of "little people" a couple of miles from the main debris field. On the day after this interview, Whitmore took Brazel to KGFL and called the Roswell Army Air Field. The military came to the station, took custody of Brazel, and confiscated the recording of Brazel's interview, made the previous evening.

The Former RAAF Guest House, South Side (Photo by E.J. Wilson)

Brazel was taken from the KGFL offices to the RAAF guest house, where he was reportedly held under armed guard for five days. Once located northwest of the intersection of South Main Street and West Byrne Street, the guest house is unfortunately no longer there. After being held in this building by the military, Brazel's story about what he saw at the Foster Ranch changed dramatically.

During his stay at the guest house, Brazel was taken under military escort to the offices of the *Roswell Daily Record* with a "revised" story about his discovery of the debris at his ranch. With his military escort standing close by, Brazel now made his discover sound more like conventional, man-made materials, such as rubber, tinfoil, paper, and wooden sticks. Also, Brazel now said that he had originally discovered the debris on June 14, instead of on July 4, as he had previously said. Although the story was sounding quite a bit different now, he did state that the debris was totally unlike what he had found when two weather balloons had crashed on his ranch previously.

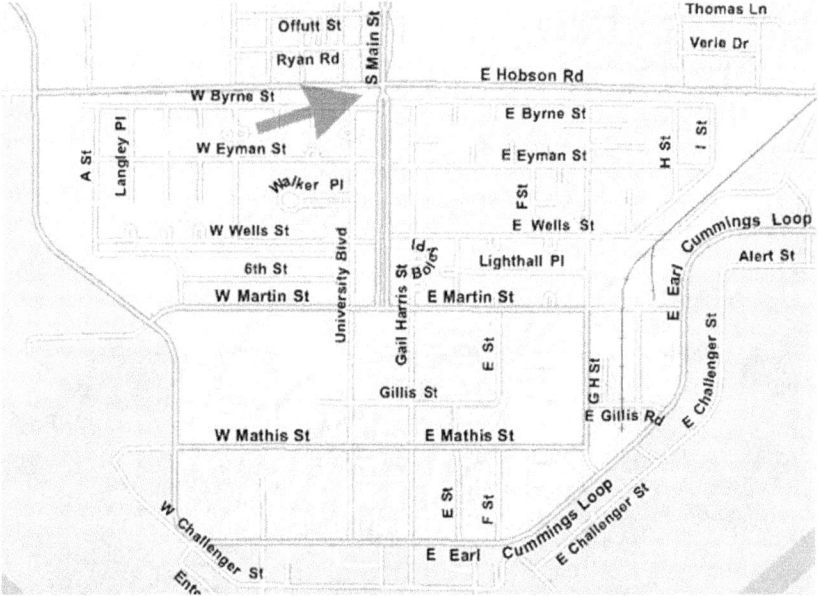

Former Guest House is at S. Main St. & Hobson Rd. (Southwest Corner)

Brazel was then taken by his military handlers to radio station KGFL, where he was permitted to go into the building by himself to speak to Frank Joyce, while the soldiers waited outside. As he started to tell Joyce the "revised" version of his story, Joyce interrupted him and asked why he had changed his story. Agitated, Brazel replied, "It'll go hard on me."

After the KGFL interview, Brazel was escorted by the military back to the guest house at the air base, where he would remain for nearly a week. During this time, he was reportedly interrogated for long hours and was subjected to an unwelcome and highly invasive physical examination. The military may also have used certain "brainwashing" techniques to try to keep him from ever talking about his experience. It was also during Brazel's confinement at the guest house that a task force of at least 60 soldiers descended upon the Foster Ranch and reportedly cleaned up every scrap of evidence that something had crashed there.

When Brazel was finally released, he refused to say anything other than that he had found a weather balloon. Privately, he complained of being mistreated by the military during his time at the RAAF guest house. He said that he was not even allowed to call his wife. He also told his children that he had to swear an oath not to talk about the incident.

Within a year after these strange events, Brazel moved back to his hometown of Tularosa, New Mexico, where he operated a refrigerated meat locker rental business. From then until he passed away in 1963, he never again spoke publicly about what happened in July 1947.

The Former RAAF Guest House, East Side (Photo by E.J. Wilson)

EIGHTEEN: BLANCHARD RESIDENCE

Status: Still standing.
Location: 1 Walker Place
Accessibility: Private residence.
GPS Coordinates: 33.318005, -104.526411.

If the Roswell Incident did unfold as described by so many witnesses, base commander William H. Blanchard stood squarely in the middle of the entire operation. According to Walter Haut, Blanchard was fully involved in the recovery of a crashed UFO and alien bodies. Blanchard also reportedly took Haut on a quick tour of Building 84, where he allowed the lieutenant to view the metallic, egg-shaped saucer and two bodies that Haut later described as being four-feet tall.

William H. Blanchard (USAF Photo Archives)

The Former Blanchard Residence (Photo by E.J. Wilson)

Blanchard's residence at the Roswell Army Air Field still stands at the end of the circular street known as Walker Place. As we visit this key location in the Roswell story, we cannot help but imagine what wonder and fear must have gripped Colonel Blanchard in July 1947, as he struggled with the orders that he was given by higher command. What thoughts and feelings must have surged through his mind late at night as he lay in his bed here, while less than a mile away, a flying vehicle from beyond the Earth and the bodies of its occupants reportedly lay on the floor of Building 84? Unfortunately, the secrets that Blanchard knew died with him on May 31, 1966.

Blanchard, a native of Boston, Massachusetts, began his military career as a graduate of the U.S. Military Academy at West Point in 1938. After completing pilot training at Randolph and Kelly fields, Texas, in 1939, the Boston native served as a flight instructor and as chief of advanced pilot training in the Flying Training Command, before becoming part of the very first B-29 bomber wing at Salina, Kansas, in 1943.

In 1944, Blanchard, then deputy commander of the 58th Bomb Wing, flew the first B-29 into China and took part in strategic bombing operations against the Japanese mainland. He flew low-level fire raids against major Japanese targets while serving as commander of the 40th Bomb Group (B-29) and then as operations officer of the 21st Bomber Command in the Marianas.

From 1946 Roswell Army Air Field Yearbook (Courtesy of HSSNM)

At the climax of World War II, Blanchard drew the assignment of preparing and supervising the operation to deliver the first atomic bomb on Hiroshima, Japan. The experience gained in atomic bombing operations led Blanchard to be named commander of the 509th Bombardment Wing, during which he served at the Roswell Army Air Field. It was during this time of his life that he came face-to-face with the Roswell Incident. Given his training and experience in atomic warfare, the most important and highly-classified military operation of its time, Blanchard was certainly qualified to manage the dangerous and volatile scenario of a UFO crash near Roswell, the retrieval of debris and bodies, and the subsequent cover-up.

Another View of the Former Blanchard Residence (Photo by E.J. Wilson)

In fact, some researchers suggest that because he did his job so well in 1947, Blanchard rose to the higher echelons of the military afterward. In 1948, he was assigned to Strategic Air Command's Eighth Air Force Headquarters as director of operations, where he helped direct the atomic training of crews for B-36s, America's first intercontinental bombers. After commanding B-50 and B-36 bomber units of SAC, he was assigned as deputy director of operations for the Strategic Air Command in 1953. Thus, the man that some UFO skeptics have said would not have been able to carry out such an effective cover-up of something as important as the Roswell Incident, was one of the key players in America's nuclear strike force during the Cold War, literally having his finger on the nuclear trigger button.

In fact, Blanchard assumed command of SAC's Seventh Air Division in England in 1957 and then in 1960 became director of operations for SAC. Obviously, he had the experience, background, and intelligence to accomplish a military cover-up on the level that has been suggested took place in Roswell in 1947.

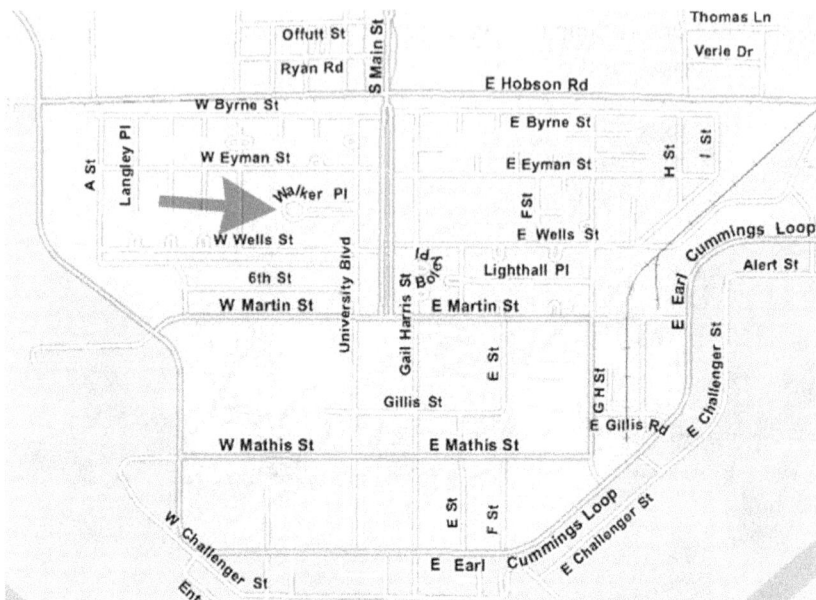

USGS Map Showing Blanchard's Former Residence

After 15 years of continuous service in SAC, he was appointed the inspector general of the U.S. Air Force and was promoted to the rank of lieutenant general. In 1963, he was named deputy chief of staff at U.S. Air Force Headquarters, and in 1965, General Blanchard became vice chief of Staff of the U.S. Air Force, with promotion to four-star rank. By this time, Blanchard had become one of the most important men in the U.S. military.

Another View of the Former Blanchard Residence (Photo by E.J. Wilson)

The residence of Colonel Blanchard during his time at the Roswell Army Air Field can be visited by heading south from Roswell on Main Street all the way to the intersection of Eyman Street. Turn west on Eyman, immediately south on University Boulevard, and then west again on Walker Place. Drive to the highest point of the circle to view Blanchard's former home. According to author Lynn Michelsohn, rumors have circulated over the years of a vast network of underground tunnels here at the former Roswell air base, with at least one tunnel supposedly connecting Colonel Blanchard's home to the RAAF control tower.

While visiting, please keep in mind that this is a private residence. Everyone is reminded to respect the property rights and privacy of the current residents. In other words, do not trespass, and do not bother the owners.

NINETEEN: ROSWELL AAF HOSPITAL

Status: Demolished. Now an empty lot.
Location: Intersection of E. Wells Street and Ruohonen Place
Accessibility: Publicly accessible vacant lot.
GPS Coordinates: 33.317157, -104.52035.

Our next stop is the vacant lot where the Roswell Army Air Field Hospital stood in 1947. It was a one-story building located one block east of the intersection of Gail Harris Street and East Wells Street. Although there isn't much to look at now, this was where Glenn Dennis said he saw UFO wreckage and also where he saw a nurse who later told him that she saw the bodies of the UFO occupants.

Vacant Lot Where Base Hospital Stood (Photo by E.J. Wilson)

In his 1991 affidavit, Dennis stated, "I got a call to transport a serviceman who had a laceration on his head and perhaps a fractured nose. I gave him first aid and drove him out to the base. I got there around 5:00 p.m. Although I was a civilian, I usually had free access on the base because they knew me. I drove the ambulance around to the back of the base hospital and parked it next to another ambulance. The door was open and inside I saw some wreckage. There were several pieces which looked like the bottom of a canoe, about three feet in length. It resembled stainless steel with a purple hue, as if it had been exposed to high temperature. There was some strange-looking writing on the material resembling Egyptian hieroglyphics. Also, there were two MPs present."

Glenn Dennis (Courtesy of Kevin D. Randle)

Dennis continued assisting the injured soldier into the building, and after checking him in with the hospital staff, he went to the staff lounge to have a soft drink and to look for a young nurse that he had previously met and chatted with. While headed toward the lounge, Dennis saw the nurse, a 23-year-old second lieutenant in the Army, coming out of one of the medical examination rooms, holding a cloth over her mouth. Noticing him standing there, the nurse said, "My gosh, get out of here or you're going to be in a lot of trouble," and quickly disappeared into another room.

When he talked to her on the following day, she told him that she had entered one of the examination rooms at the hospital to get some medical supplies out of a storage area, when suddenly she realized that she had walked into the middle of a very strange autopsy being conducted by two military physicians. They were conducting a preliminary autopsy on three beings that were clearly not human. "She said she had never smelled anything so horrible in her life, and the sight was the most gruesome she had ever seen," Dennis said.

Vacant Lot Where Base Hospital Stood (Photo by E.J. Wilson)

Nauseated by the smells and sights in the room, she was hoping to turn and quickly leave, but the doctors motioned her over and instructed her to take notes during the procedure. Focusing her attention once more at the strange creatures on the tables before her, she became fully convinced that they were not any form of life from planet Earth. "This was something no one has ever seen," she later told Dennis.

Of the three bodies lying on tables in the room, three were "very mangled and dismembered," as if predatory animals had damaged them as they lay in the desert prior to being recovered by the military. One of the bodies was "fairly intact," according to the nurse. As the nurse spoke to Dennis, she took a slip of paper and began drawing a diagram of the bodies. She described the beings as about three and a half feet tall with a disproportionately large head, deeply-set eyes, concave nose with two holes, a narrow slit for a mouth, and ears consisting of a small hole with a flap of skin. The creatures had no hair at all, and their skin was black, possibly from exposure to the sun after the crash. Instead of teeth, they had heavy cartilage, and their skulls that were "flexible" rather than rigid. The nurse's attention was especially drawn to the hands of the creatures, which had only four fingers with each finger having a pad resembling a suction cup at the end.

Drawing by Walter Henn Based on Sketch Seen by Glenn Dennis

As the examination continued, she heard one of the doctors say, "This isn't anything we've ever seen before. There's nothing in the medical textbooks like this." Overcome by nausea and revulsion, both she and the doctors became ill and vomited during the procedure. The doctors requested that the hospital's air conditioning system be turned off so that the smells would not permeate throughout the building.

In the end, a decision was made to stop the autopsies and move the bodies out to an airplane hangar, presumably Building 84, before examining them further. Other witnesses later testified to seeing a makeshift morgue and the strange bodies inside Building 84.

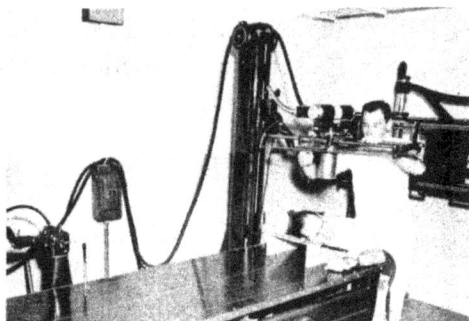

1940s Photo of RAAF Hospital Examination Room (HSSM)

Dennis did not learn any of these facts during his brief visit to the hospital. Instead, after his brief conversation with the nurse during which she suggested that he leave right away, he was approached by a stern-looking Army captain. The captain asked Dennis to identify himself and state his purpose for being in the hospital.

Dennis explained about bringing in the injured airman, and then he attempted to engage the captain in conversation about what was going on around him. Dennis told him, "It looks like you've got a crash; would you like me to get ready?" The captain told Dennis to stay right where he was and then turned and left him. Moments later, two military policemen appeared and told Dennis that he had to leave and that they had been instructed to escort him all the way back to Ballard Funeral Home. At that point, they began to forcefully remove him from the base hospital and out the back door. On the way out, Dennis was approached by another captain, which he later described as "a redhead with the meanest-looking eyes I have ever seen." Also with him was an African-American sergeant holding a notepad in one hand. The captain told the MPs, "We're not through with that SOB. Bring him back." The captain came up to Dennis and said, "You did not see anything. There was no crash here. And, if you say anything, you could get into a lot of trouble." Dennis responded, "Hey look mister, I'm a civilian and you can't do a damn thing to me."

"Yes, we can," the captain answered, "Somebody will be picking your bones out of the sand." At that point, the sergeant with the notepad added, "He would make good dog food for our dogs," and the captain said, "Get the SOB out."

Vacant Lot Where Base Hospital Stood (Photo by E.J. Wilson)

The MPs followed Dennis back to the funeral home, and he heard no more about the strange happenings at the air base until the next day. More curious than ever, Dennis tried to call the nurse he had previously talked to in the hospital, but he was unable to get through to her.

At about 11 a.m., Dennis was still on the job at Ballard Funeral Home when the nurse called him and said simply, "I need to talk to you." They agreed to meet at the Roswell Army Air Field Officer's Club, as will be discussed in the next chapter.

The RAAF hospital building has unfortunately been demolished. The empty lot where the building once stood is near the intersection of East Wells Street and Ruohonen Place. Immediately northwest of this site is where the hospital for Walker Air Force Base stood from 1960 until the base closed in 1967. It later housed the New Mexico State Rehabilitation Center (NMRC) and now has been demolished. It is eerie to stand on this ground and think back to the alleged recovery of alien bodies and the medical examinations that were reportedly performed at this very place.

This undated photograph shows the Walker Air Force Base Hospital, which later became the NMRC. (HSSN)

Interestingly, when the NMRC occupied the adjacent buildings, some ghostly sightings were recorded there, according to Roswell author John LeMay, who recently wrote the following account of the facility's eerie goings-on:

Speaking of aliens, the most extraordinary sighting of some-thing strange at the NMRC happened to Josephine

Morones who saw what she calls the "little man." Others call it the "Alien Ghost."

In July 1997, when interest in the Roswell Incident was peaking due to the 50th anniversary celebration, Morones, stepped out of the staff kitchen one night and was struck by a very odd sensation. Turning to look down the hall, she saw the most bizarre sight of her life - a small figure that looked somewhat human but clearly was not.

"My thing was very weird. The hands weren't like fingers; they were like mittens. All I could see was the thumb. The skin, or whatever it had on, was like silk tape. We have [silk tape here] and it looked to me like someone wrapped up in that silk tape," said Morones of the figure. When asked whether or not she thought it looked like an alien, she said, "It had the egg/pear shaped head. You know how people talk about the slanted eyes and all of this? This one had round eyes. That's what really got me. It didn't have a nose; as far as a mouth it had a little bitty mouth. At first, I thought somebody was playing a trick on me. I really did. I couldn't explain the feeling."

As she watched the figure, her body went stiff with fear, and she was unable to move. Morones noted that the figure cast no reflection in the glass cabinet it was standing in front of at the end of the hall. "I kept looking at it and I didn't panic because I've known about this place for a long time…but I looked at the glass expecting to see a reflection and what got me was there was no reflection. I kept looking at it and it suddenly just faded out and then I was able to move," said Morones.

She saw the figure again several nights later. "I was walking out of the kitchen and I got that feeling again and that time I knew what it was. With that in mind I was able to turn around and look and it was just standing there again."

This time Morones was able to call for a coworker to come and look at it too, but by the time she finished calling him, the figure had disappeared. It has not been seen since.

In summing up her strange encounter, Morones said, "The first time it freaked me out and I was really afraid. I had heard all these stories and stuff, but I never really believed them. I didn't feed into stuff like that. I didn't believe in all the stuff that was going on this building."

For some, the fact that the sighting took place during the time of the Roswell Incident's 50th Anniversary arouses some suspicion. However, it should be noted that Morones never once sought publicity for her sighting and, if anything, actually shunned the spotlight. Morones told only her fellow NMRC staff workers (who had seen plenty of strange things themselves in the building). Among those she told was the assistant to the executive director, Jacqueline Allen. Allen said she and the nurses were discussing the alien festivities and mentioned how fascinating it would be to actually see a real alien, when Morones first came forward with the story of her strange sighting.

It should also be noted that Morones herself has never uttered the words "alien ghost." She calls what she saw "the little man."

Some years later, the NMRC was chosen as a filming location for a documentary Jim Marrs was making on the Kennedy Assassination. "The reason for filming in Roswell is simple." wrote Jim Marrs in an article entitled "Alien Ghosts at Roswell?" for his official website, "The people are friendly and cooperative, the climate is generally dry, costs are much lower that other parts of the country, and the place is a treasure trove of old items from years past -- clothing, cars, military equipment."

It was at the NMRC while working on the documentary that Marrs first heard about the alien ghost sightings and later brought them to light on the Internet. While Marrs spoke to Jacqueline Allen about filming in a storage area on the second floor of the NMRC, Allen told him that most employees felt that particular wing of the hospital was haunted. This piqued the curiosity of Marrs, who is also an investigator of the paranormal. As the conversation continued, Allen told Marrs about Morones's sighting in July 1997.

Marrs then interviewed several of the night workers (although it is not clear if he interviewed Morones in person) while working on the documentary, and thus, word of the "alien ghost" got out. Morones was later contacted for an interview, and unbeknownst to her, it was recorded and broadcast on a paranormal radio program.

The always reliable *Weekly World News* even headlined their March 26, 2007 cover with "Alien Ghost Haunts Roswell!" (Other gems published by the paper included the "Alien skull found at Roswell" and Oprah's efforts to buy Area 51.) This particular headline is not entirely inspired by events at the NMRC, though. It seems Joshua P. Warren, a paranormal investigator, held a séance at Hangar 84 in an effort to talk to one of the dead aliens! He did this as research for Jim Marrs' cancelled *X-Ops* series for the Discovery Channel. Warren further said that a high-definition camera used during the experiment recorded a "large snake-like figure" floating around the hangar. Make of that what you will.

Visitors to the area where the old RAAF hospital stood are asked to observe all warning signs and are cautioned not to trespass into any of the adjacent buildings. Park only in designated parking zones, and be aware of your personal safety at all times.

TWENTY:
RAAF OFFICERS' CLUB

> *Status:* Now the Eastern New Mexico University Campus Union Bldg.
> *Location:* 48 University Boulevard
> *Accessibility:* Public building owned by Eastern New Mexico University.
> *GPS Coordinates:* 33.314607, -104.524798.

The former officers' club building at the Roswell Army Air Field is now the Campus Union Building (CUB) for Eastern New Mexico University at Roswell. The building contains a college cafeteria, which is open to the public. Visitors may enjoy a snack or a meal while considering the mysterious events that took place here in July of 1947. For it was in this building that Glenn Dennis met with the nurse he had seen in the hospital the night before. It was here that the nurse told Dennis that she saw three non-human bodies being autopsied.

Campus Union Building, Formerly the Officers' Club (Photo by E.J. Wilson)

1940s Photo of the Officers' Club (Courtesy of HSSNM)

The nurse called Dennis at the Ballard Funeral Home earlier in the day and set an appointment to meet him at the officers' club. After they both arrived at the club, Dennis noticed that the nurse was pale, and he was concerned that she was on the verge of going into shock. "She was very upset," Dennis later remembered. "She said, 'Before I talk to you, you have to give me a sacred oath that you will never mention my name, because I could get into a lot of trouble.' I agreed."

Sitting together at a quiet table in the officers' club, the nurse proceeded to tell him about the incredible events from the night before. As she told her story of seeing the three alien bodies undergoing a preliminary autopsy, she took a slip of paper and began drawing sketches of the creatures she had seen.

When she finished telling Dennis her story, she gave him the drawings that she had made. Dennis took them and then drove her back to the officers' barracks. Although he did not realize it at the time, Dennis would never see the young nurse again.

The Former Officers' Club near Intersection of University Blvd. & Martin St.
(U.S. BLM Map)

When he tried to reach her at the hospital the next day, Dennis was told that she was not available. He continued trying to reach her for several more days, until another nurse told him that she and several others of the base's medical personnel had been "transferred out."

A couple of weeks later, Dennis received a letter from the nurse. It had an APO (military postal service) number for a return address. In the letter, she told Dennis that she wanted to discuss by mail more about what she had seen in Roswell. Encouraged, Dennis wrote back to her; however, his letter was returned to him two weeks later, and it was stamped, "Return to Sender – DECEASED." Afterward, Dennis learned of a rumor that the nurse had been killed in a plane crash, along with five other nurses, during a training exercise.

Like many of the other Roswell witnesses, Dennis felt pressure from authorities never to reveal what he experienced during the Roswell incident. Chaves County Sheriff George Wilcox, who was a personal friend of Dennis' parents, showed up at their home after the events at the base and said to Dennis' father, "I don't

108

know what kind of trouble Glenn's in, but you tell your son that he doesn't know anything and hasn't seen anything at the base." Wilcox also said that the military had requested the names and addresses of all members of the Dennis family.

Recent Photo of Former Officers' Club (Photo by E.J. Wilson)

Immediately after the visit from the sheriff, Dennis' father went straight to the Ballard Funeral Home and asked Glenn for an explanation of what exactly he had seen at the base. He told his father everything that took place, including the nurse's story. According to Dennis, his father was the only person to whom he told the story until around 1990 when he was contacted by researchers working on several books about the Roswell Incident.

Also in the 1990s, Dennis attempted to find the sketches that the nurse had made of the alien bodies. He had stored them at the Ballard Funeral Home in his personal files. Unfortunately, over the years, the sketches, along with many of his other papers from the 1940s, had been cleared out and thrown away.

If you would like to visit the former officers' club building at the Roswell Army Air Field, fortunately it is one of the most accessible of the buildings that are connected to the Roswell Incident. As a cafeteria designed for students attending Eastern New Mexico University at Roswell, the building is now an enjoyable place to pause for a meal or refreshments.

During the 2010 Roswell UFO Festival, authors Noe Torres and E. J. Wilson offered walking tours of the old Roswell Army Air Field, starting at the Campus Union Building. As each tour began, the authors told participants about the mysterious events that unfolded in the building back in 1947.

Another View of the Campus Union Building (Photo by E.J. Wilson)

TWENTY-ONE:
RAAF WATER TOWER

Status: Still standing and still in use.
Location: 122 E. Earl Cummings Loop
Accessibility: City government property.
GPS Coordinates: 33.312065, -104.515195.

One of the eeriest stories related to the Roswell Incident occurred in the unlikeliest of places – on East Earl Cummings Loop right in front of the Roswell Army Air Field water tower. According to the story, the lieutenant governor of New Mexico in 1947, Joseph Montoya, called his lifelong friend, Ruben Anaya, and requested that Anaya bring a car and meet him at the water tower outside Building 84. "Get your car, Ruben, and pick me up. Get me the hell out of here," Montoya said, according to accounts given later by Anaya.

Joseph Montoya (left) and RAAF Water Tower with Building 84 in Background (right)

111

Anaya, along with his brother Pete and a friend named Moses Burrola, drove as requested to the water tower, where they found Lieutenant Governor Montoya standing by the road waiting for them in a very agitated and frightened state. As he got into the car, Montoya's first words were, "Get me the hell out of here. I want to go." He was extremely pale, shaking, and seemed very scared.

1940s Photo Looking to the East, Showing Water Tower
(Courtesy of HSSNM)

On the drive out of the base, Montoya said nothing, still struggling to compose himself, but once they reached their destination, according to Ruben Anaya, the lieutenant governor began talking. "You all are not going to believe what I've seen. If you ever tell anyone, I'll call you a damned liar. We don't know what it is. They say it moves like a platter. It's a plane without wings. It's not a helicopter. I don't know where it's from. It could be from the moon. We don't know what it is."

Montoya went on to relate the extraordinary scene he had witnessed inside Building 84. He claimed to have seen four "little men," one of whom was obviously still alive, because it kept "moaning." The beings were "short ... skinny like with big eyes. [The] mouth was real small, like a cut across a piece of wood."

The creatures had been put on mess hall tables inside the hangar, and a team of doctors were crowding around each table, engaged in examining the beings.

Water Tower with Building 84 in Background (Photo by E.J. Wilson)

Pete and Ruben Anaya recalled Montoya saying that the beings were very skinny and did not appear at all like human beings. They were hairless, had white skin, unusually large eyes, and wore tight-fitting one-piece suits. They had four long, thin fingers on each hand. The Anaya brothers kept asking Montoya questions about the mysterious creatures, until at one point, Montoya blurted out, "I tell you that they're not from this world."

Montoya, who went on to become a powerful and influential member of the U.S. Senate for many years (1964-1977), never publically commented on what he saw in Roswell, if anything. The entire "water tower" story thus is second-hand testimony from Pete and Ruben Anaya, who waited until the 1990s, well after the death of their friend Montoya, before finally telling the story. However, friends and relatives have acknowledged that the Anayas and Montoyas were close acquaintances, and it seems unlikely to many researchers that the Anayas would betray their friendship to Montoya after his death by fabricating a false story about him.

Water Tower Still Stands outside Building 84 (Photo by E.J. Wilson)

TWENTY-TWO: BUILDING 84

If there is a deep, dark center to the Roswell universe, it has to be the uncanny and mysterious Building 84, located on East Challenger Street. Also known as Hangar P-3, this building, according to a number of witnesses, became a makeshift morgue in July 1947, where military doctors reportedly examined three dead non-human entities and one still living that were recovered from a crashed UFO somewhere north of Roswell.

1940s Photo of Building 84 (HSSN)

115

In an affidavit filed in 1991, former Roswell mortician Glenn Dennis told of the air base nurse who inadvertently walked into an examination room at the base hospital as two military doctors were conducting a preliminary autopsy on three non-human bodies that presumably were recovered at the UFO crash site north of Roswell. The nurse was horrified by the smells and sights of the unearthly bodies, and after she was asked by doctors to stay and take notes for them, she became ill, as did both doctors, from the stench. At that point, the nurse later told Dennis that the doctors decided to move the autopsy area to "one of the aircraft hangars," presumably Building 84, based on the testimony of other witnesses, including the Anayas and the base public information officer in 1947, Walter Haut.

The Imposing Structure of Building 84 (Photo by E.J. Wilson)

In a 2002 affidavit, Haut remembered the eerie sight he beheld inside this building on the afternoon of July 8, 1947. As Colonel Blanchard walked him toward Building 84, Haut observed that the hangar was under "heavy guard" both outside and inside. Blanchard ushered Haut into the building and allowed him to gaze upon a scene that he would carry deep within his psyche for the rest of his life. "Once inside, I was permitted from a safe distance to first observe the object just recovered north of town. It was approx. 12 to 15 feet in length, not quite as wide, about 6 feet high, and more of an egg shape. Lighting was poor, but its surface did appear metallic. No windows, portholes, wings, tail section, or landing gear were visible.

Inside of Building 84 (Photo by E.J. Wilson)

Haut also noticed two bodies under a canvas tarpaulin. "Only the heads extended beyond the covering, and I was not able to make out any features. The heads did appear larger than normal and the contour of the canvas suggested the size of a 10-year-old child. At a later date in Blanchard's office, he would extend his arm about four feet above the floor to indicate the height."

The statement closes with Haut saying that he was told about a temporary morgue set up to accommodate the recovered bodies and was also told that the UFO wreckage was not radioactive. He ended the affidavit by stating, "I am convinced that what I personally observed was some type of craft and its crew from outer space."

A few years ago, author E. J. Wilson visited Building 84, under lease to Stewart Industries International, LLC, of Guthrie, Oklahoma. Stewart Industries uses the old RAAF hangar to dismantle airplanes that are being scrapped for parts. An employee showed Wilson around the facility, allowing him to take as many photos as he wished and providing an informal tour of perhaps the premier site in Roswell lore.

Southwest End of Building 84 (Photo by E.J. Wilson)

As Wilson walked around the building taking pictures, the employee confirmed that she and her colleagues are well familiar with the stories about what happened here inside this very building. Standing inside the cavernous hangar with its high arching roof, we were struck by the realization that Walter Haut claimed to have seen the crashed UFO and two alien bodies right here where we stood. Pausing for a moment, one can almost feel a strange mental and physical connection with the events that happened so long ago in this eerie place.

The employee then took Wilson to another very strange place, located deep inside Building 84, where legend has it that the alien bodies were kept by the military, after they were recovered at the UFO crash site north of town. Stewart Industries employees call it the "gray" room, which may refer to the drab color of the room or the "gray aliens" that were supposedly held there in July 1947.

The Small Room Inside Building 84 Where the Bodies Were Kept
(Photo by E.J. Wilson)

The room is tiny and is now used for general storage. Sunlight streams in through the windows as one walks around the cramped space and wonders what strange sights were seen here during the height of the Roswell Incident. It makes sense that the shockingly unusual UFO occupants would be kept securely out of view in this tiny room within the dark recesses of the massive aircraft hangar at this former Army air base. It is a strange sense of wonder and awe that fills the visitor to this most unusual of places.

If you are interested in visiting Building 84, please keep in mind that Stewart Industries strictly enforces a "no trespassing" policy and does not offer tours of their facility to the general public. Given the nature of the work that Stewart employees perform, the presence of tour groups could create potentially dangerous situations for the visitors. Tours would definitely raise liability concerns with the company's insurers and would tend to generally interfere with the company's work at the facility. Nevertheless, visitors are free to look around and take pictures from outside the fenced area of the facility, alongside Challenger Street.

The Gray Room (Photo by E.J. Wilson)

Many persons familiar with the Roswell Incident have long expressed a desire that Building 84 be set aside as a special historical site, rather than having it continue to be used for industry. Perhaps this will happen one day soon.

The authors would like to express sincere appreciation to Stewart Industries for allowing us to visit and photograph Building 84. For more information about this innovative company, please visit *www.siiair.com*. Stewart is one of the leading suppliers of aviation spare parts in the heavy jet industry. At its warehouse facilities in Oklahoma, the company houses millions of FAA-approved spare parts for various Boeing, Airbus, Lockheed, and McDonnell Douglas aircraft. At its Roswell facility, the company dismantles aircraft that have gone out of service and have been sold by the airlines as scrap.

The Roswell Air Center is a popular storage area for jet aircraft that are temporarily out of service or are waiting to be scrapped for parts, as the arid climate is known to help preserve the craft. When visiting the former military air base, you will notice large numbers of diverse aircraft, representing many airlines, all parked on the old RAAF tarmac, basking in the Roswell sunshine.

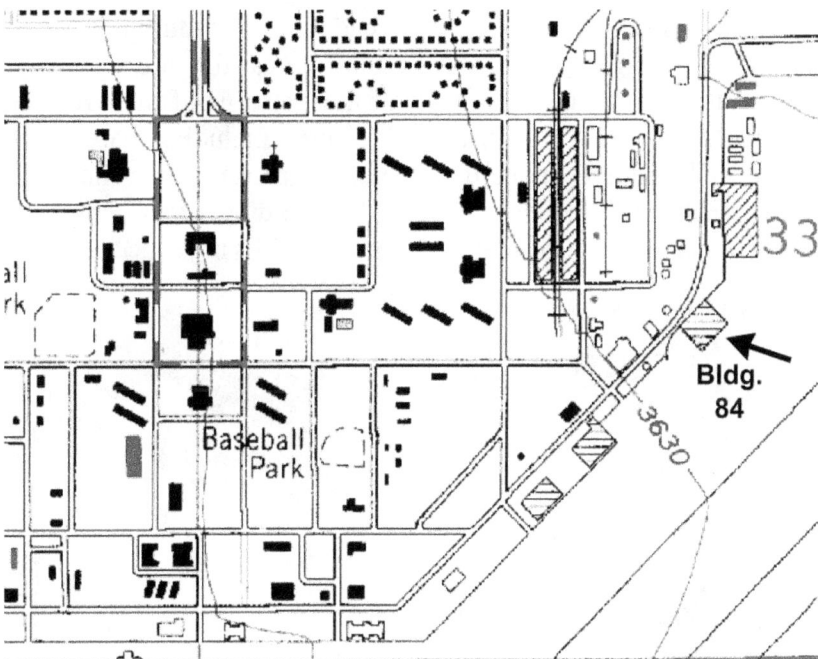

1962 Map Showing Location of Building 84 (USGS)

TWENTY-THREE:
RAAF HEADQUARTERS

Status: The base headquarters is no longer standing.
Location: Now an empty lot, NW of the intersection of Gail Harris and Gillis Streets
Accessibility: Unfenced. Publicly accessible vacant lot.
GPS Coordinates: 33.312665, -104.523363.

The Roswell Army Air Field headquarters building is unfortunately no longer standing. A vacant lot near the intersection of Gail Harris and Gillis Streets is all that remains of the structure where the RAAF brain trust held court, including base commander William Blanchard and public information officer Lt. Walter Haut. It is believed that in this building, Haut composed the famous press release about a "captured" flying saucer.

1960s Photo of Old Headquarters Building (Courtesy of HSSNM)

The office of Major Jesse Marcel Sr., meanwhile, was most likely at the headquarters of the 509th Bomb Group, a building that was located closer to the flight line, south of the base headquarters. In 1947, this was the nerve center of the world's first nuclear strike force, with Blanchard as commander, Haut as his public information officer, and Marcel as the intelligence officer. After all, this was the division that coordinated the dropping of the first atomic bomb on Hiroshima.

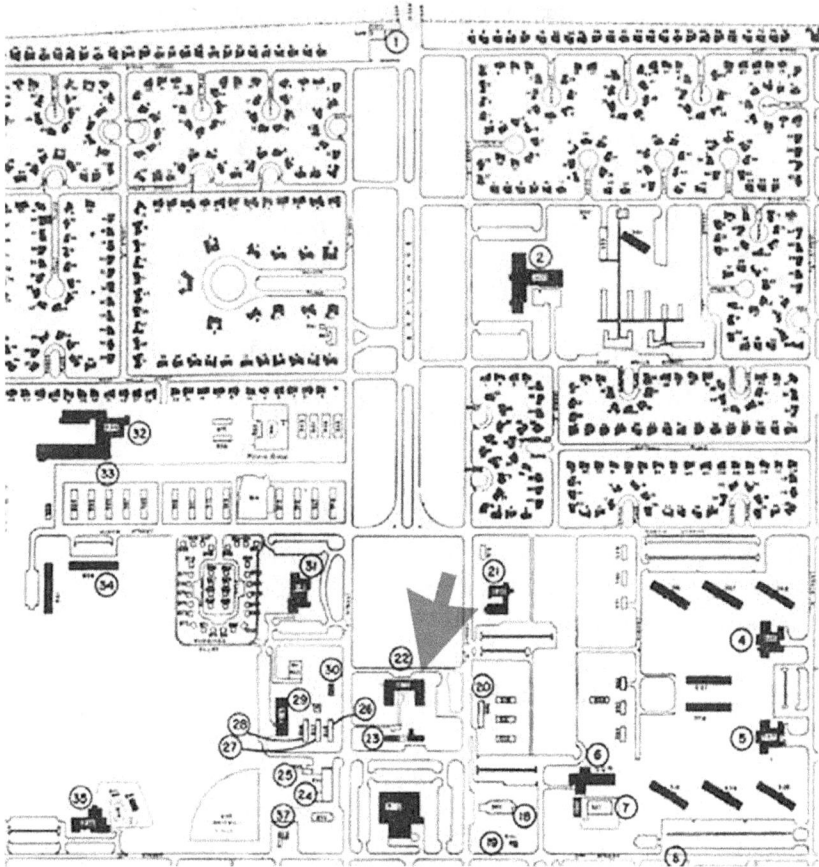

The Former RAAF Headquarters Building

Regarding his famous "captured saucer" press release, Haut said, "Col. Blanchard told me to write a news release about the operation and to deliver it to both newspapers and the two radio stations in Roswell. He felt that he wanted the local media to have the first opportunity at the story. I went first to KGFL, then to KSWS, then to the *Daily Record* and finally to the *Morning Dispatch*."

The text of Haut's original press release was simple and straightforward, but from n those few words, he suspected that a firestorm would erupt. The press release said:

> The many rumors regarding the flying disc became a reality yesterday when the Intelligence office of the 509th Bomb Group of the Eighth Air Force, Roswell Army Air Field, was fortunate enough to gain possession of a disc through the cooperation of one of the local ranchers and the sheriff's office of Chaves County.
>
> The flying object landed on a ranch near Roswell sometime last week. Not having phone facilities, the rancher stored the disc until such time as he was able to contact the sheriff's office, who in turn notified Maj. Jesse A. Marcel of the 509th Bomb Group Intelligence Office.
>
> Action was immediately taken, and the disc was picked up at the rancher's home. It was inspected at Roswell Army Air Field and subsequently loaned by Major Marcel to higher headquarters.

The day after Haut's press release went out, the Army put out its famous retraction. Haut said, "The next day, I read in the newspaper that General Roger Ramey in Fort Worth had said the object was a weather balloon.

"I believe Colonel Blanchard saw the material, because he sounded positive about what the material was. There is no chance that he would have mistaken it for a weather balloon. Neither is there any chance that Major Marcel would have been mistaken.

"In 1980, Jesse Marcel told me that the material photographed in Gen. Ramey's office was not the material he had recovered. I am convinced that the material recovered was some type of craft from outer space."

As you visit the vacant lot where the RAAF base headquarters building once stood, think about the tremendous impact that the decision to release the "captured saucer" story had on that world that day in 1947. That brief statement typed by Haut, under the direction of Colonel Blanchard, is very likely the world's foremost UFO document. Its ramifications were immense and continue to be felt today, as people study the incredible events of that period. The former RAAF headquarters stood just south of the big empty lot that served as the parade grounds.

Empty Lot Where Base HQ Stood (Photo by E.J. Wilson)

TWENTY-FOUR: RAAF FIRE STATION

Status: Still standing.
Location: 10 West Challenger St.
Accessibility: Private property.
GPS Coordinates: 33.306761, -104.523599.

In a story that first came to light in March 2009, a 90-year-old former Roswell city fireman, identified only as "Mr. Smith," told an amazing story about the involvement of both the city and RAAF fire departments in the retrieval of a crashed UFO somewhere north of town. Smith, who was interviewed by investigators Anthony Bragalia and Kevin Randle, is the only member of the 1947 Roswell fire department who was still alive as of 2009.

Former RAAF Fire Station (Photo by E.J. Wilson)

Smith told Bragalia and Randle that immediately after the UFO crash happened, a very tough-spoken Army colonel visited the Roswell Fire Department and told the firemen that an "unknown object from someplace else" had crashed in the desert outside town. He emphasized to them that the "rescue" operation was being handled entirely by military personnel, and that the city firefighters should not attempt to go out to the scene of the crash. Further, he told them to keep quiet about the crashed object. Because of what the colonel said to the Roswell firefighters and also what he later heard from other witnesses, Smith is convinced that an object not from Earth did indeed crash north of Roswell in July 1947.

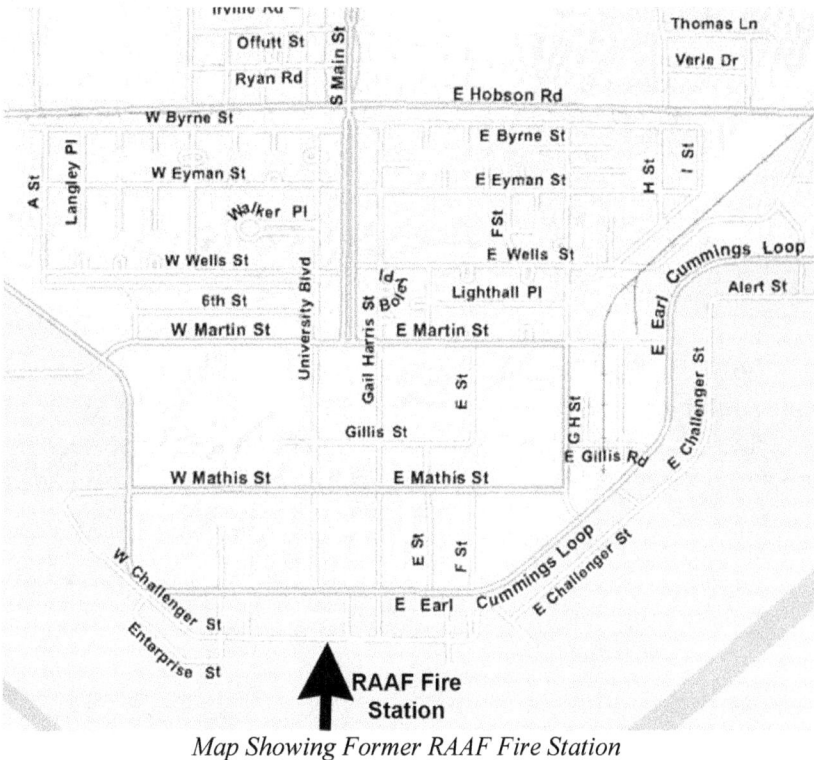

Map Showing Former RAAF Fire Station

Regarding the role of Roswell firefighters in the UFO incident, Smith said that it was actually the Roswell Army Air Field's own fire department that was most involved in the crash recovery and clean-up process. It was the RAAF firemen who "knew the most" about what happened. Although several city firefighters, including Dan Dwyer, defied the colonel's orders and went out to the crash site on their own, they were not asked to go and were not formally involved in the operation, according to Smith.

Another View of Former RAAF Fire Station (Photo by E.J. Wilson)

Located south along the flight line, the RAAF fire station had three large garage bays for fire fighting vehicles and a tower to overlook the runways. When visiting this building, please heed all posted notices and warnings. Be sure to park only in designated parking areas.

TWENTY-FIVE: RAAF FLIGHT OPERATIONS

Status: Still standing.
Location: 4 East Challenger St.
Accessibility: School district property. Restricted access.
GPS Coordinates: 33.306873, -104.52264.

In their book *Witness to Roswell*, Tom Carey and Don Schmitt tell the incredible story of Robert J. Shirkey, who in 1947 was a lieutenant at the Roswell Army Air Field, serving as assistant operations officer for the 509th Bomb Group. Shirkey was the officer on duty at the RAAF Flight Operations building on July 8, 1947, when he witnessed a very strange procession of men and materiel pass by close to where he was standing.

Former RAAF Flight Operations Bldg. is Now a School
(Photo by E.J. Wilson)

Just outside the flight operations building, a B-29 bomber stood ready for take-off to Wright Field in Ohio, as Shirkey saw Colonel William Blanchard, the base commander, enter the building. After confirming with Shirkey that the B-29 was ready for takeoff, Blanchard signaled a group of men to enter the building and proceed to the waiting B-29. Shirkey saw Major Jesse Marcel, Sr. and at least six unidentified men wearing dark blue suits (perhaps FBI agents) move into the main hallway of the flight operations building. Because Colonel Blanchard seemed to be deliberately standing in a manner that blocked his view, Shirkey asked Blanchard if the colonel would mind moving a bit. After Blanchard moved slightly, Shirkey was able to see that Marcel and most of the other men were each carrying an open cardboard box filled with what Shirkey later described as "scrap metal." The material looked like non-reflective aluminum.

Shirky, Robert, 1st Lt.
Photo from 1946 RAAF Yearbook (Courtesy of HSSNM)

As Marcel carried his open box past him, Shirkey's gaze fell upon an extremely strange sight. "Sticking up in one corner of the box ... was a small I-beam with hieroglyphic markings on the inner flange, in some kind of weird color, not black, not purple, but a close approximation of the two," Shirkey told Carey and Schmitt.

The strange procession of men headed on out to the tarmac, hoisted the boxes up through an open hatch in the B-29, and then all the men boarded the plane. "Here it came, and there it went," Shirkey said. "That's all I saw."

Apparently, though, what he saw was enough to derail his military career for a time. Shortly after the strange events in Roswell, Shirkey was inexplicably transferred to a base in the Philippines, where he was assigned to a job that did not exist. Reporter Stephen Johnson of the *Houston Chronicle* summarizes the strange circumstances of Shirkey's sudden transfer away from Roswell:

> Shortly after this event, Shirkey, who was awaiting promotion to Captain and assignment to a new job at Roswell air base, shortly afterward received some startling news.
>
> "Nine days later I got a telegram from the Eighth Air Force sending me to Clark Field in the Philippines to fill the request the 13th Air Force had made for a weights and balance officer," said Shirkey.
>
> His orders, oddly enough, were signed by Brigadier General Roger Ramey, the Eighth Air Force commander who ordered Marcel to pose next to the debris that Marcel said was not what he had recovered.
>
> When he [Shirkey] arrived at Clark Field in the Philippines he had another surprise when he was informed that no such job vacancy existed.
>
> Shirkey was told the 13th Air Force had a weights and balance officer and didn't need one. He would instead be made assistant operations officer in a photo reconnaissance unit.

As far as Shirkey was concerned, his inexplicable departure from Roswell "was part of the cover-up" of the saucer crash. As it turned out, his request that Colonel Blanchard move slightly so that he could look at what was being loaded onto the plane may have cost him in terms of his military career.

UFO investigators looking into the Roswell case maintain that Shirkey was not the only soldier to suddenly be transferred far away from New Mexico soon after July 1947, as also happened to the Army nurse who Glenn Dennis claimed had witnessed an autopsy being performed on an alien body recovered at the crash site.

The H-shaped building that served as RAAF Flight Operations still stands today at 4 East Challenger Street, located immediately to the east of the old RAAF fire station. In 1947, this building was where incoming and outgoing flights were managed. It was here that Army aviators received their orders for missions, filed their flight plans, and received briefings about their missions. It was here, too, that aircraft were made ready for flight and were then dispatched for take-off, under the guidance of the RAAF air traffic control. Upon returning from a mission, flight crews would be de-briefed in this building as well.

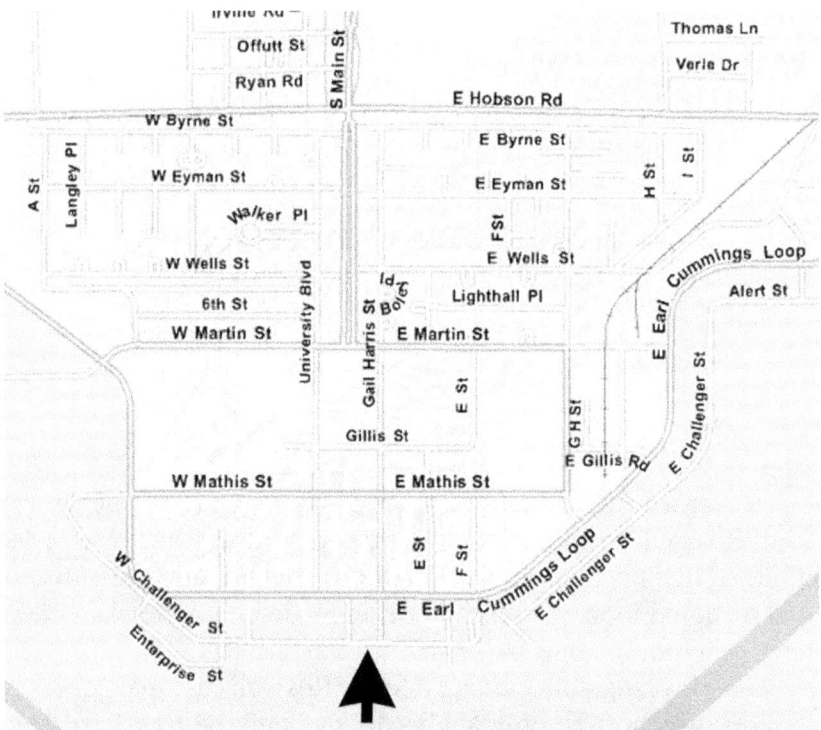

Arrow Shows Location of Former RAAF Flight Ops

The former Flight Operations Building is now the Sidney Gutierrez Middle School, named after a retired NASA astronaut, and is part of the Roswell Independent School District. Tours of the school building are not available to the general public, and visitors that do not have school-related business are not allowed on campus during school hours, due to the school district's security procedures. Members of the public who would like to visit this site will be able to see only the exterior of the building. We recommend stopping by on a weekend or on any day when school is not in session.

If you would like to contact the school, call (575) 627-8357. The school's Web site is *www.sgms.us*. It may be possible to schedule a tour of the building on a day when school is not in session and district staff is available to escort visitors; however, such arrangements must be made with school district officials in advance of any such tour.

Sidney Gutierrez Middle School (Photo by E.J. Wilson)

Status: Incinerator unit was demolished circa 1999.
Location: Near intersection of S. Aspen Rd. & Old Y O Crossing Rd.
Accessibility: Airport property. Fenced. Restricted access.
GPS Coordinates: 33.287243, -104.547321.

The former incinerator unit for the Roswell Army Air Field is a fascinating site for a number of reasons. The incinerator, shown in the historical photo below, operated from 1941 until 1967 and was used to destroy classified documents and other materials. Located on the extreme southwest corner of the RAAF, this was also the site where one witness, at the time of the Roswell Incident, saw a large Army tent surrounded by an 8-foot-tall chain-link fence.

RAAF Incinerator Unit (U.S. Government Photo)

As reported to Carey and Schmitt, the eyewitness, Corporal Edward Harrison, was ordered to take a detachment of soldiers under his command and post them around the mysterious tent that had suddenly appeared in one of the most remote corners of the air base – the southwest edge. Harrison and his men were told to "shoot anything that isn't a rabbit."

1940s Photo of RAAF - Arrow Points to the Southwest Corner of the Base
(Courtesy of HSSNM)

Harrison left his men to carry out their overnight assignment, and when he returned to check on them the following morning, he was amazed to find that the tent and the 8-foot-tall fence had disappeared without a trace. Later in life, as Harrison heard more about the Roswell Incident, he became convinced that he witnessed part of a military operation to hide the bodies recovered at the Roswell UFO crash prior to transporting them away from Roswell by plane.

Carey and Schmitt theorize that bodies from the crash were kept at this remote location due to the incredibly strong smell that had earlier caused medical personnel to nearly faint at the base hospital. According to this theory, sometime before dawn, the bodies were moved from the makeshift tent on the southwest edge of the air field onto a nearby section of runway. Then, the bodies were loaded onto a Boeing B-29 aircraft using a hydraulic lift normally used to load bombs onto planes. To any distant observers, the early morning activity on the runway would not have attracted much attention, as cargo being loaded onto planes was a common site at the RAAF.

Another interesting aspect of the incinerator is that it may well have been used to dispose of documents pertaining to the 1947 Roswell Incident. Given the scope of the retrieval and cover-up operation, it seems reasonable to assume that the military would have generated a large body of classified documents detailing the event. At a later date, these documents were likely burned in the RAAF incinerator to ensure that the military's secret Roswell files would never be read by the general public.

Photo of Roswell Army Air Field from 1946 RAAF Yearbook
(Courtesy of Historical Society for Southeast New Mexico)

Located southwest of the runways, the incinerator site is, even today, extremely isolated and not frequently visited. To reach the site, go south on Main Street from the center of town until you reach the entrance to the Roswell Air Center. Go right on W. Hobson Road, heading west until the road turns south and becomes S. Nevada Road and then later becomes S. Aspen Road. Continue on Aspen until it ends at the intersection of Old Y O

Crossing Road. You are now at the site of the former RAAF incinerator station. The area is fenced, and you will have to look in from outside the fence.

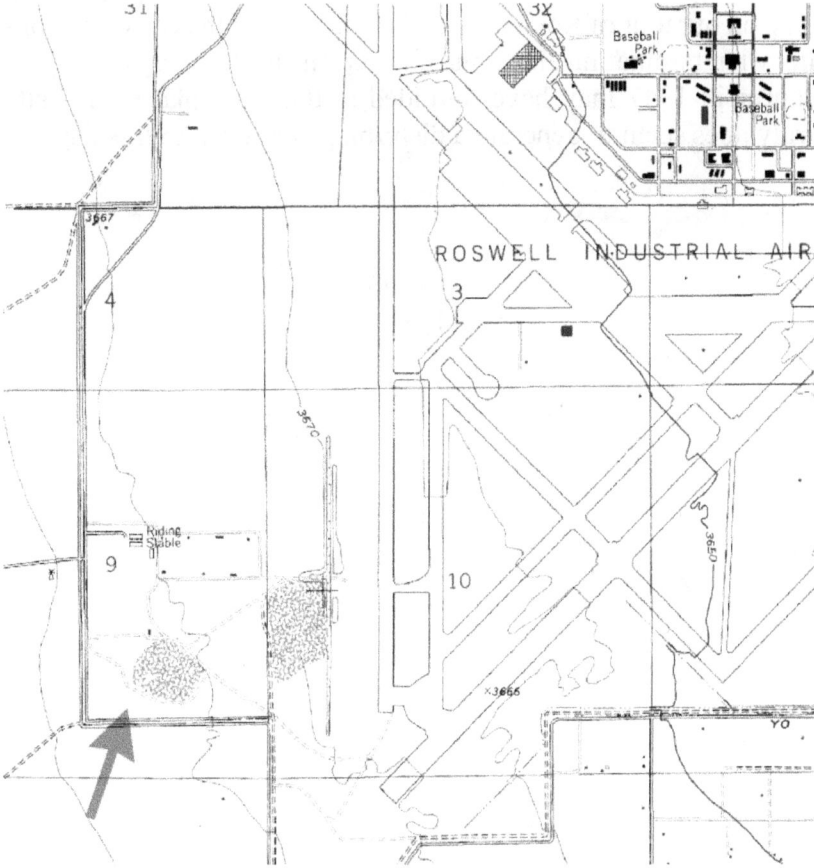

Arrow Shows Former Incinerator Site (Courtesy USGS)

When visiting this area, please keep in mind that the roads are subject to closure due to airport activities. Please exercise great caution when visiting this area. Heed all warning signs. Do not impede any airport operations. Respect barriers, including fences. If asked to turn back by authorities, please do so immediately. Do not enter areas that are clearly off-limits to the general public. Remember that security around airports has become a very important concern in the past few years.

The former incinerator site is certainly another spellbinding stop on our tour of Roswell's UFO landmarks. One can only wonder what fascinating elements of the crash and recovery of a flying saucer in 1947 may have unfolded at this very place. This site truly does seem to generate a disturbing aura even to this day.

TWENTY-SEVEN:
WOODY FARM &
MILITARY CORDON

Status: Ranch is privately owned land. Roadway is public.
Location: 6400 Cree Road, Dexter, NM, and then north on Highway 285.
Accessibility: Private property. Public access along roadside.
GPS Coordinates: (Former Woody Farm) 33.299704, -104.46049.

In a sworn affidavit given on September 28, 1993, another Roswell resident stated that he saw a very unusual sight in the skies over Roswell on or around July 4, 1947. The witness, William M. Woody, was 13 years old at the time and living on his family's farm, located three miles south of Roswell, just east of the Roswell Army Air Field.

Woody and his father were standing outside "well after sundown," when they saw something incredible, according to the affidavit: "Suddenly, the sky lit up. When we looked up to see where the light was coming from, we saw a large, very bright object in the southwestern sky, moving rapidly northward.

"The object had the bright white intensity of a blow torch, and had a long, flame-like tail, with colors like a blow-torch flame fading down into a pale red. Most of the tail was this pale red color. The tail was very long, equal to about 10 diameters of a full moon.

"We watched the object travel all the way across the sky until it disappeared below the northern horizon. It was moving fast, but not as fast as a meteor, and we had it in view for what seemed like 20 to 30 seconds. Its brightness and colors did not change during the whole time, and it definitely went out of sight below the horizon, rather than winking out like a meteor does. My father thought it was a big meteorite and was convinced it had fallen to earth about 40 miles north of Roswell, probably just southwest of

139

the intersection of U.S. Highway 285 and the Corona road (State Highway 247).

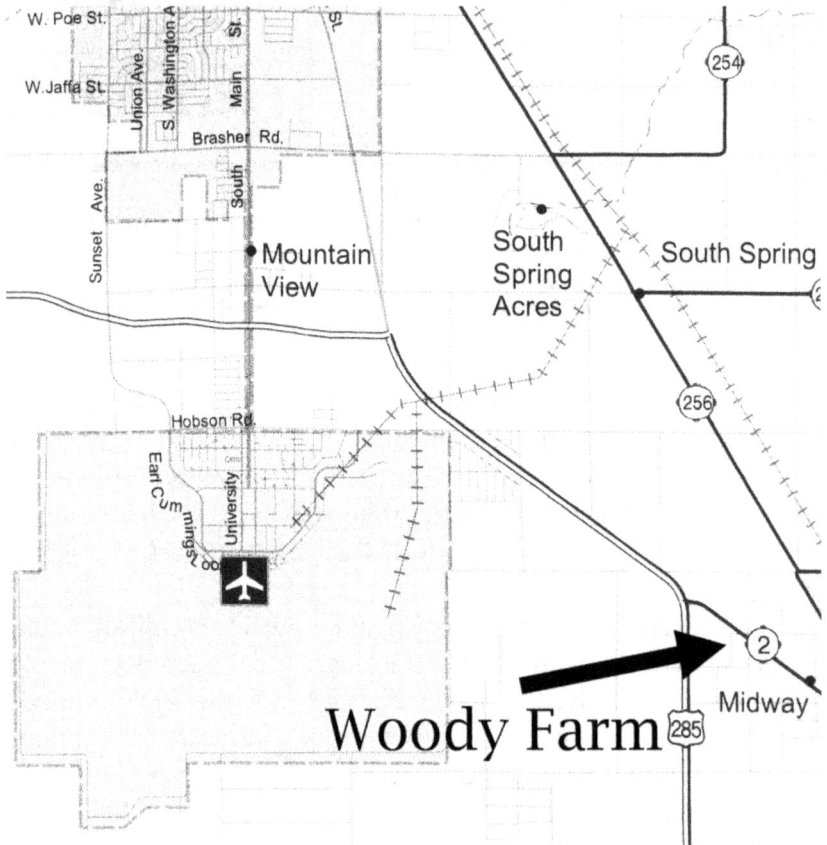

William Moody Observed UFO from His Family's Farm Southeast of Roswell (NM-DOT Map)

The point from which the Woodys observed the UFO is located in the 6400 block of Cree Road, which now falls within the town of Dexter, New Mexico. Interestingly, their observation of a bright object moving from the south toward the north on the west side of Roswell is consistent with what was reported by the Franciscan nuns at St. Mary's Hospital.

Believing that the object had fallen somewhere along Highway 285 north of town, Mr. Woody and his son later got in their farm truck and headed north on 285, hoping to find out more about what they had witnessed. What they found instead was a strong military presence with orders not to let any civilians near the crash site.

The Former Woody Farm (2011 Photo by E. J. Wilson)

William Woody remembered that he and his dad took to the road shortly after witnessing a very bright object zoom over their heads at the Woody Farm moving rapidly from the south to north. "My father thought it was a big meteorite and was convinced it had fallen to earth about 40 miles north of Roswell, probably just southwest of the intersection of U.S. Highway 285 and the Corona road [State Highway 247]."

Although the elder Woody was very curious about the object, other concerns intruded, and he waited "two or three" days before deciding to travel north of town to try to find where the "meteorite" hit. "My father knew the territory, all its roads, and many of the people very well, so two or three days later (definitely not the next day), he decided to look for the object. He took me with him in our old flatbed truck. We headed north through Roswell on U.S. 285."

William M. Woody (2011 Photo by Sharalee Trudeau)

As the Woodys headed north out of town, they suddenly became aware of a military presence along Highway 285. The soldiers were posted as "sentries" to keep curious civilians from exiting Highway 285 and taking any of the roads leading into the desert to the west, toward Socorro. "About 19 miles north of town, where the highway crosses the Macho Draw, we saw at least one uniformed soldier stationed beside the road," William Woody testified. "As we drove along, we saw more sentries and Army vehicles. They were stationed at all places - ranch roads, crossroads, etc. - where there was access to leave the highway and drive east or west, and they were armed, some with rifles, others with side arms." The description is clearly that of a large-scale operation designed to keep the curious away from the vicinity.

Many UFO researchers have made the point that if the military was simply guarding the wreckage of an experimental high-altitude balloon, why would they post so many guards along all the roads leading into the desert north of Roswell? Similarly, if the only thing they were guarding was some strange debris at the Foster Ranch, located near Corona, why would they be sealing off all desert roads along Highway 285 so much closer to Roswell? To many, the heavy military presence seen by the Woodys is a strong indication that something more significant than a balloon had crashed somewhere in the desert north-northwest of Roswell, that it was something more noteworthy than just the Foster Ranch debris, and that it was, in fact, a crashed saucer and bodies. The military was taking definitive action to insure that as few people as possible found out about the so-called "final impact site," where the UFO and bodies were found.

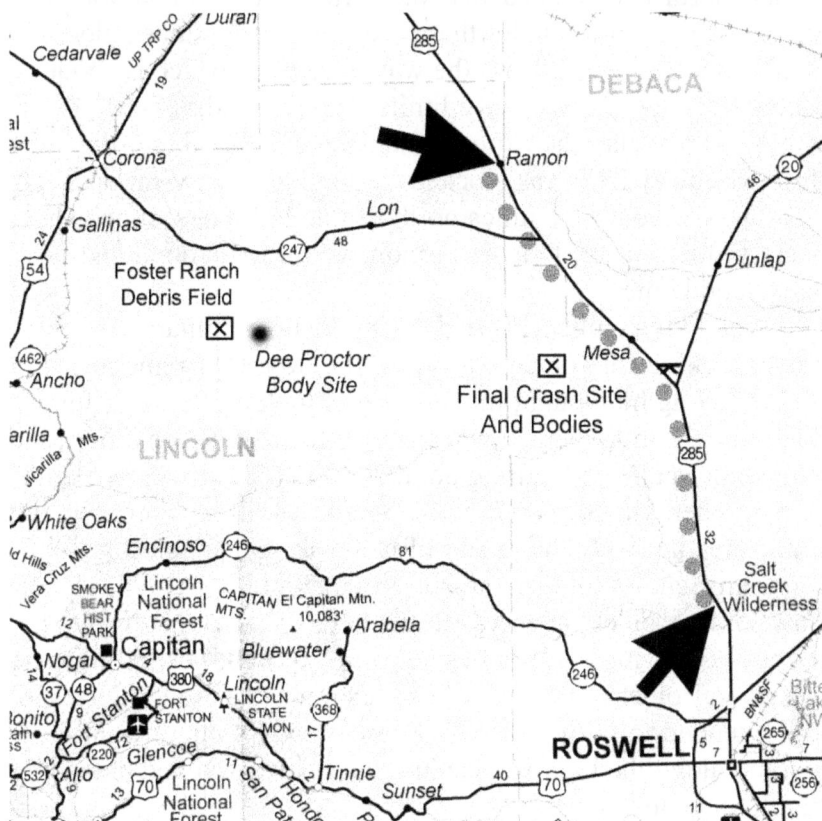

Location of Military Cordon, Relative to Suspected Crash Sites
(NMDOT Map)

After noticing all the guards, William Woody and his dad stopped to inquire about the situation. "We stopped at one sentry post, and my father asked a soldier what was going on. The soldier, whose attitude was very nice, just said his orders were not to let anyone leave 285 and go into the countryside." Clearly, researchers say, the soldiers were not told what they were guarding, or perhaps they were told that a secret government airship had crashed in the desert. Most of the Roswell Army Air Field soldiers to this day have no idea what their assignment was really about on that day in July 1947. All they have heard are rumors and insinuations, of which they themselves have no direct knowledge.

Woody and his father continued driving along Highway 285 to the north and noticed that the turn off to Corona was also blocked by the military. Furthermore, soldiers continued blocking exits from Highway 285 all the way to Ramon, which is about 60 miles from the Roswell city limits. Woody said, "As we drove north, we saw that the Corona road (State 247), which runs west from Highway 285, was blocked by soldiers. We went on as far as Ramon, about nine miles north of the 247 intersection. There were sentries there, too. At Ramon we turned around and head south and home."

Woody remembers his dad saying that the military was obviously looking for something out in the desert. "I remember my father saying he thought the Army was looking for something it had tracked on its way down. He may have gotten this from the soldier he spoke with during our drive up 285, but I am not sure."

Another witness also reported seeing a military cordon in the same area in 1947. University of Nebraska paleontologist Dr. C. Bertram Schultz told researcher Kevin Randle in 1993, that he saw soldiers blocking access to the desert west of Highway 285, as he was driving 15-20 miles north of Roswell. Schultz was one of several other witnesses whose testimony, although less specific, tended to corroborate William Woody's tale of a military cordon along the highway leading out of Roswell and extending north to the town of Ramon.

The Highway 285 cordon site can be viewed on the way to the Foster Ranch debris field, starting about 10 miles north of Roswell and continuing all the way to the turnoff for Highway 247. Imagine the military manpower it must have taken to seal off all exits from this highway.

TWENTY-EIGHT: FOSTER RANCH DEBRIS FIELD

Status: Public land.
Location: Approx. 99 miles northwest of Roswell, near Corona, NM.
Accessibility: U.S. government property but surrounded by private land.
GPS Coordinates: 33.945385, -105.308553.

About a 99-mile drive northwest of Roswell, at the J. B. Foster Ranch near Corona, New Mexico, rancher William Ware "Mack" Brazel was listening to roaring thunder from a violent electrical storm over his ranch on the evening of July 4, 1947. Suddenly, he heard one particularly loud explosion that was distinctly unlike any of the other thunder booms. The same unusually loud explosive sound was also heard by a number of other residents of the area near the Foster Ranch.

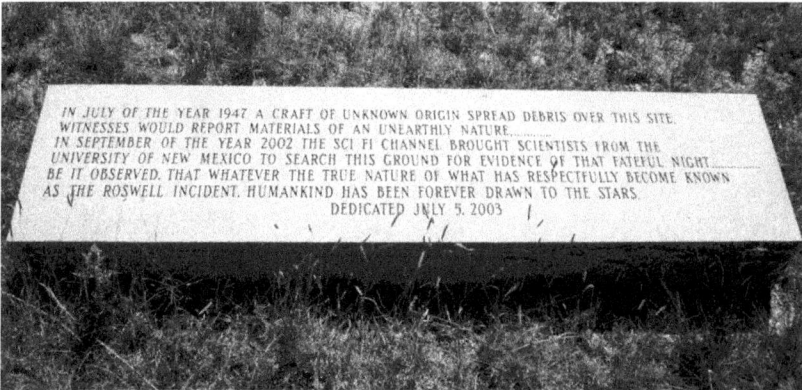

Marker Placed Near Foster Ranch Debris Field (Photo by E.J. Wilson)

On the following morning, while surveying the ranch to see the storm's effects, Brazel found a large debris field consisting of strange metallic fragments. Many UFO researchers believe the

145

fragments were pieces of the flying saucer that had sustained damage during the violent electrical storm.

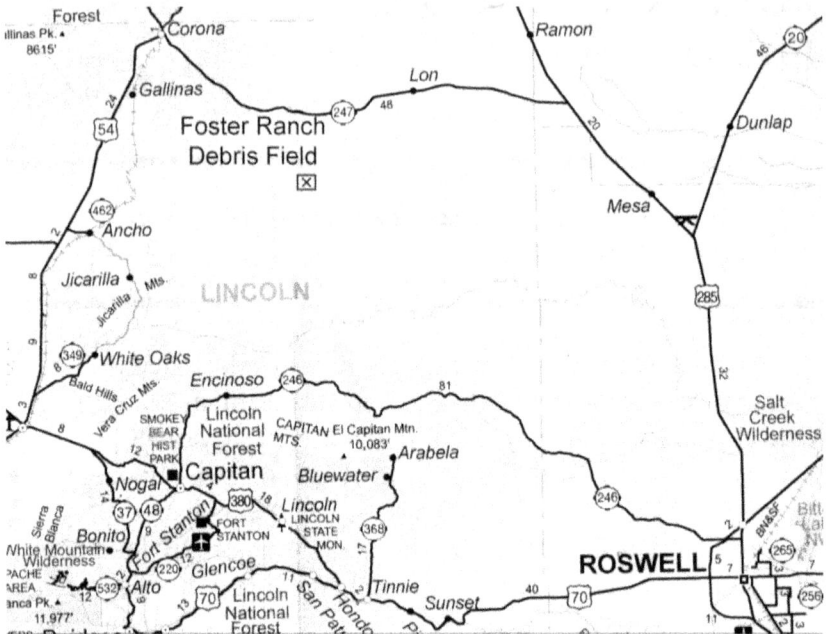

The Foster Ranch Debris Site is Marked (NMDOT Map).

Although the Foster Ranch is only one of several "crash" locations that have been linked to the July 1947 UFO incident, this is the only one that everyone agrees on – even skeptics. That there was a field of unknown debris found at the Foster Ranch during the first week of July in 1947 is a universally accepted fact. To believers, the debris field was created by metallic fragments from a UFO. To non-believers, it was debris from an experimental high-altitude balloon array designed to detect Russian nuclear tests, or it was some other man-made object.

How to Get There

Caution: Do not attempt this trip without extra food, water, basic survival gear, a four-wheel drive vehicle that has good ground clearance and a driver with experience on rough terrain.

Wear appropriate protective clothing, including boots, to help protect against rattlesnakes. Additionally, there is minimal cell phone signal, habitations, or infrastructure of any kind. If you get there and your vehicle doesn't start, you will be walking quite some distance back to B007 to get help. You are responsible for proper preparation and your own safety.

Disclaimer: The authors have made every effort at providing accurate coordinates but cannot be responsible for technical errors (i.e. your mileage may vary).

Directions from Downtown Roswell

1. Go NORTH on Main St (NM 285-N) until you pass Wal-Mart on the left.
2. Turn LEFT onto W. Pine Lodge Rd (NM 246-W) at 33.452261, -104.523642.
3. Continue WEST on W. Pine Lodge, (NM 246-W) 4.2 miles. At 33.451773, -104.594415, follow the curve right to stay on NM-246.
4. Continue on NM-246 another 54.9 miles, staying on NM-246 all the way to B007/Transwestern Rd. at 33.710025, -105.360991. You will see signs on your right which indicate the Corona 8 Compressor Station, immediately followed by a street sign "TRANSWESTERN." This is where you turn RIGHT. Note: Transwestern is also referred to as T/W.

1. CONTINUE 16.7 miles to intersection with an old landing strip at 33.922401, -105.332205. The old landing strip is perpendicular

to the road and looks like old, broken asphalt, as shown in the photos below.

2. From the landing strip, proceed slowly exactly 2.5 miles and stop. On your right, you should see a tire-track trail which looks like the photo below. Turn RIGHT onto it. The GPS coordinates for the start of this trail are: 33.95802, -105.33236.

The Trail Leading to the Roswell UFO Crash Marker

CAUTION: The trail gets rough, and at some locations, you are driving on and across some very rocky ravines and dry stream beds.

Carefully follow the trail 1.7 miles to the Sci-Fi (now SyFy) Channel plaque and rock monument on your left, pictured below at 33.945385, -105.308553. Congratulations, you have arrived!

From where the plaque and monument are, looking to the east-southeast, you will see, off in the distance, a windmill tower assembly, standing next to a water tank and a corral. Going to that location, which is an optional part of our trip, will put you a bit closer to the area where the largest concentration of UFO debris was found on the Foster Ranch by Mack Brazel back in 1947.

The Windmill and Corral Seen in the Distance

Although the debris was scattered over a very large area, a large grouping of it was found closer to the windmill and corral location. To get there, from the Sci-Fi Channel marker and stone monument, continue along the trail for another .7 miles to the east-southeast, until you reach the area of the windmill. In the following photographs, you will see the approach to, and arrival at, the windmill location, which is located at the following GPS coordinates: 33.94287, -105.297208.

Arrival at the Windmill and Corral

Although the old Foster Ranch location now sits on public land managed by the U.S. Bureau of Land Management (BLM), it can only be reached by traveling across stretches of privately owned land. Permission should be obtained from the property owners in advance of any visit. For more information about how to access this land, please contact the Roswell Field Office of the Bureau of Land Management, at 2909 W. 2nd Street in Roswell. Their phone number is (575) 627-0272.

When traveling to the debris field site, members of the public are urged to respect all signs and fences put up by private land-owners in the area and to abide by all federal regulations regarding public access to BLM lands. Federal law prohibits "defacing, disturbing, destroying or removing personal property, structures, livestock, archaeological resources, mineral resources or any natural resources." There are also a number of other important laws and restrictions, about which more information can be obtained from the Roswell Field Office of the BLM.

Noe Torres and John LeMay at the site of the historical marker erected by the SyFi Channel (left) and the stone marker (right). A view of the area (below).

Given its high significance to everyone searching for truth about the Roswell case, many researchers feel that the Foster Ranch location should be protected for future generations. The site is still the subject of a number of ongoing investigations about the 1947 event, and visitors should take great care to disturb nothing at the location, to take nothing from the site, and to leave nothing behind.

Even the federal government has taken steps to protect the Foster Ranch location, according to researcher Dennis Balthaser, "I must congratulate the United States Department of the Interior, Bureau of Land Management (BLM). In a recent Environmental Assessment of the ranch where the debris site is located, the BLM protected the site in their report with the following statement: 'One of the alleged UFO crash sites of 1947 is located on this allotment. The UFO crash site has been excluded from rights-of-way and mineral leasing. The site will be withdrawn from mining claim location, and designated a NSO (No Surface Occupancy) for oil and gas leasing.' Even though the word 'alleged' is used in the BLM statement, it indicates to me, that someone within the BLM had the foresight to at least protect this property for the future."

The "Other" Crash Sites

As previously mentioned, the Foster Ranch debris field is the only "crash" site upon which everyone agrees, both UFO believers and skeptics. The believers say the debris found there was from a UFO; the skeptics say it was a conventional, manmade object like a high-altitude military balloon. So, is the Foster Ranch the one and only Roswell UFO crash site? Well, not exactly. Most UFO researchers believe that the debris found at the Foster Ranch was deposited there when the distressed UFO "bounced" or "skipped" before it regained flight and continued traveling in a roughly east-southeast direction for another 30 or 40 aerial miles before it finally slammed into the ground and was later recovered by the military. Determining where this "final impact" occurred has been one of the most elusive aspects of the Roswell Incident.

152

According to researchers Tom Carey and Don Schmitt, the Roswell UFO shed debris over the Foster Ranch, bounced, and then continued flying until it finally crashed in northwestern Chaves County approximately thirty miles east-southeast of the ranch. Along the way to its final resting place, the UFO also dumped additional debris and two or three bodies at a location known as the "Dee Proctor Body Site."

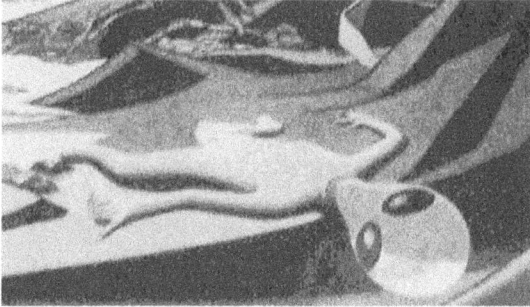

Mural at Roswell UFO Museum (2008 Photo by Noe Torres)

In their book *Witness to Roswell,* Carey and Schmitt tell the story of Timothy "Dee" Proctor, who was seven years old in 1947 and later told his mother that he was with Mack Brazel when Brazel found "something else" at a site about 2 ½ miles east-southeast of the Foster Ranch debris field. Although he never stated precisely what he saw, researchers believe that Proctor witnessed the finding of two or three non-human bodies and some additional debris from the UFO. These were the bodies that Mack Brazel supposedly spoke about during a phone conversation with KGFL radio announcer Frank Joyce on July 7, 1947.

Joyce stated in 1994 that, during the phone call, Brazel referred to the dead bodies he had found at the ranch as "little people – unfortunate little creatures" and that the "stench" from their bodies was "just awful." Joyce's testimony about what he heard Brazel say forms the basis for the theory of the "Dee Proctor Body Site." Proctor, who passed away in 2006, refused all interview requests and remained totally silent about what he witnessed.

The Dee Proctor body site is approximately 2.5 miles east-southeast of the Foster Ranch debris field, but it is not publicly accessible. The land is privately owned, and no tours are available. UFO researchers who have received special permission to visit the site report that no evidence or visible trace of any kind remains at this location.

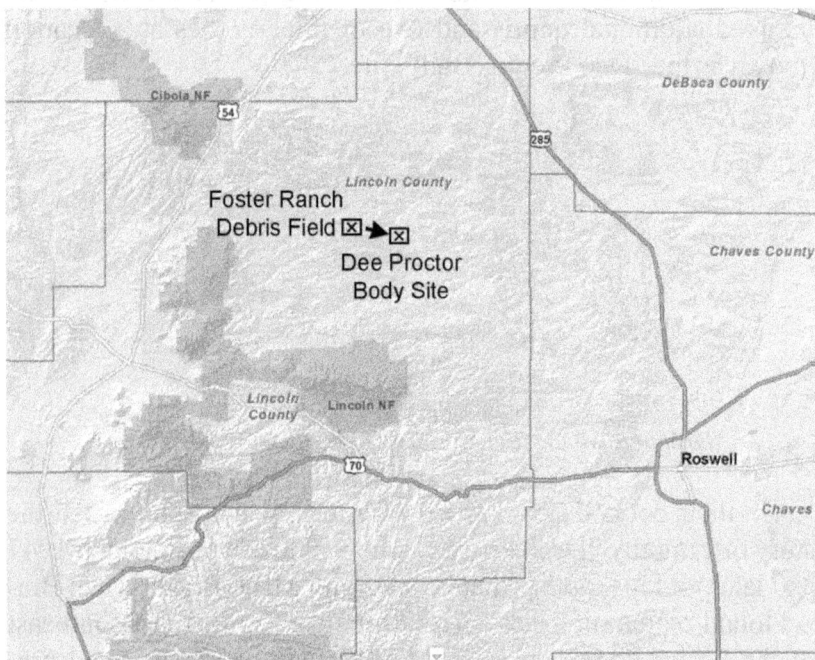

Dee Proctor Site, Approximately 2.5 miles East-Southeast of Foster Ranch Debris Field (BLM Map)

After dumping the debris and bodies at the Proctor site, the Roswell UFO apparently continued flying east-southeast into northern Chaves County, where it finally went down about 40 miles north of Roswell. A number of witnesses, including Chaves County Sheriff George Wilcox and several Roswell firemen and police officers, reported seeing a crashed flying disk and alien bodies at a location north of Roswell, not far from Highway 285.

Don Burleson, in his publication *Roswell Trajectory Feasibility*, wrote, "By all accounts, the Roswell UFO underwent some sort of disabling trauma (possibly a midair lightning strike) over the [Foster Ranch] Debris Field, scattering its debris over many acres of prairie and falling to earth somewhere down country. The real question, when one takes the Debris Field as the starting point for analysis, is then how far downrange is the object likely to have fallen?"

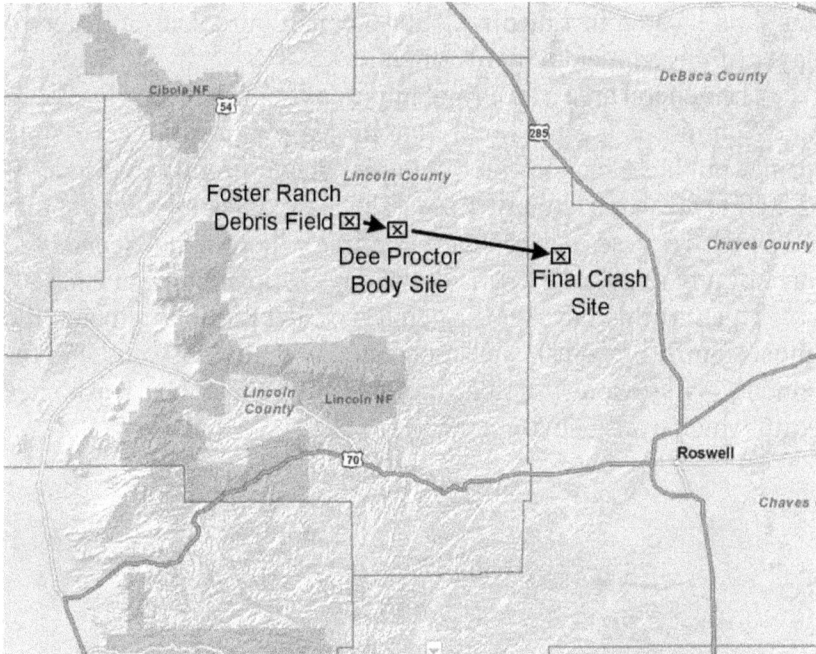

Final Crash Site, Approx. 30 mi. E-SE of Proctor Site (BLM Map)

In their book *Witness to Roswell*, Tom Carey and Don Schmitt have proposed that the object crashed for good at a location approximately 33 miles east-southeast of the Foster Ranch It is at this final crash site, according to Carey and Schmitt, that three dead non-humans and one living being were later recovered by the military. This location is approximately 40 miles north-northwest of the Roswell city limits, which correlates generally with the reported site of a crashed spaceship and bodies mentioned by a number of Roswell witnesses, including Walter Haut (in his 2002 affidavit), KSWS general manager John McBoyle, and farmer William M. Moody's father. Other witnesses, such as Texas Tech University archeologist W. Curry Holden and Army CIC Master Sergeant Lewis S. "Bill" Rickett, also mentioned a site "north of town" somewhere along Highway 285.

Notably, this proposed site is in Chaves County, the governmental seat of which is Roswell, which may explain the involvement of Roswell firefighters, police, and other officials in the crash retrieval. The Foster Ranch Debris Field, on the other hand, is located in Lincoln County, which introduces a different layer of governmental involvement.

The general area of the final impact site, as identified by Carey and Schmitt, is located on private property and is not accessible to the public. Nor does any obvious, above-ground evidence of the UFO crash exist today. Researchers are quick to point out that Roswell witnesses stated that the military thoroughly cleaned the area of any remaining debris in the days following the crash.

Thus, to this day, the Foster Ranch debris field remains the most significant "crash site" associated with the Roswell UFO Incident. As previously noted, it is the only one of the crash sites with which everyone seems to agree.

UFO Crash Diorama at Roswell UFO Museum (Photo by Noe Torres)

TWENTY-NINE: WADE'S BAR IN CORONA

> *Status:* Privately owned building.
> *Location:* 531 Main Street in Corona, New Mexico.
> *Accessibility:* Private property. No public access.
> *GPS Coordinates:* 34.249226, -105.595015.

Although Roswell is most closely associated with the UFO incident of 1947, the tiny village of Corona is actually the closest inhabited place to the Foster Ranch debris field, which is about 30 miles to the southeast. With a population of about 200, Corona remains an easily overlooked refueling stop on U.S. Highway 54.

1999 Photo of the Former Wade's Bar (Courtesy of Dennis Balthaser)

Noe Torres (left) and John LeMay (right) in front of the Former Wade's Bar

Brazel was a regular customer at Wade's Bar, which was the only such establishment in the Corona area and the closest bar to the Foster Ranch. Jesse Wade purchased the bar in 1936 and operated it until 1976, two years before his death.

Right after he discovered debris at the Foster Ranch, Mack Brazel is said to have first visited Wade's Bar in Corona to tell of what happened, before going on to Roswell. Brazel reportedly stopped by the bar and told owner Jesse Wade about what he had seen. Wade's son, Chuck, in a 2004 interview with researcher Linda Moulton Howe, said, "Mack Brazel drove up in an old pick-up truck, came up to my Dad and wanted Dad to go out to the Foster Ranch to see what in the world had crashed there."

Brazel told Jesse Wade that what fell on his ranch was "stuff he had never seen before." Deciding that he needed to stay at the bar, Wade told Brazel that he could not go. "Dad was the only person working at the bar and he chose not to close the bar and go with Mack," Chuck recalls. "Yes, Dad did later regret not going with Mack."

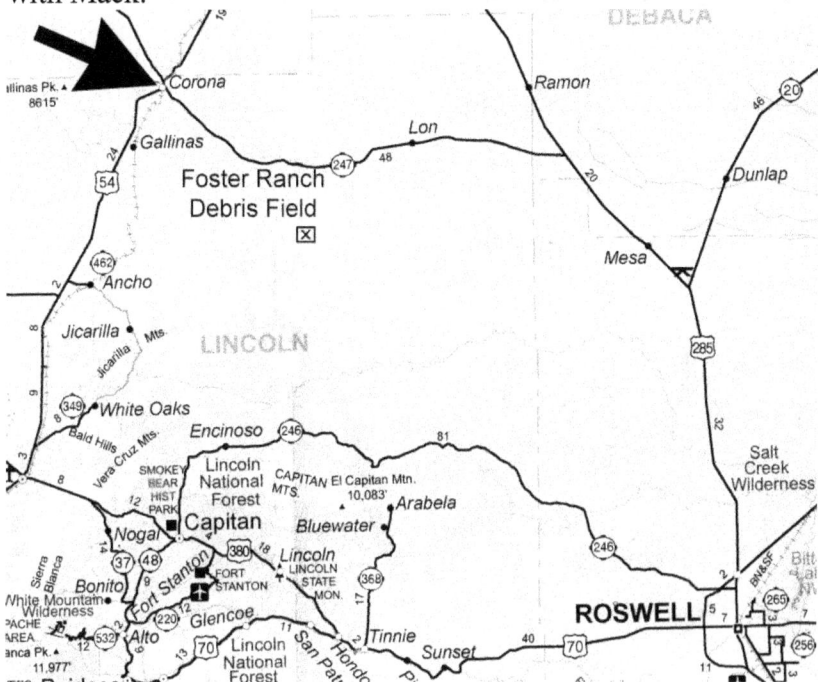

Map Showing Corona, New Mexico (NM Dept. of Transportation)

The rancher then went to the nearby Duboise Drugstore to use a phone, presumably to call somebody in Roswell and tell them about his find. This may have been the call Brazel made to Frank Joyce of KGFL radio in Roswell. Chuck Wade said, "After Mack left Dad's bar he went a few doors south to the drug store. Geraldine Perkins told me on two occasions, in the presence of her daughter Sherrill, about Mack coming in to the drug store and trying to get her husband, Archie, to go out to the Foster Ranch and see what had crashed out there. Archie did not go with Mack. Geraldine said she helped Mack make a phone call to Roswell."

Some versions of the story have Brazel actually bringing one or more pieces of the debris with him to Wade's Bar a day or two after the crash. Chuck Wade is skeptical, though. "Dad never mentioned that Mack had any of the crash material with him," Chuck said. "And Dad mentioned several times that Mack *never* spoke to him about the crash again after that first encounter." Although, according to Chuck, Mack Brazel never mentioned the strange incident again, Mack's son, Bill, did talk about it and about the strange debris found scattered around the Foster Ranch.

Recent Photo of the Building That Was Formerly Wade's Bar

In *The Roswell Incident*, Bill Brazel told the authors, "One night about two years after Dad's incident, I went into Corona for the evening. While I was there, I guess I talked too much – more than I should have. I know I mentioned having this collection [of debris from the UFO crash] to someone. Anyway, the next day a staff car came out to the ranch from Roswell with a captain and three enlisted men in it. Dad was away at the time, but it turned out they didn't want him anyway. They wanted me."

"Seems the captain - Armstrong, I think his name was, Captain Armstrong - had heard about my collection and asked to see it. Of course, I showed it to him, and he said that this stuff was important to the country's security and that it was most important that I let him have it to take back with him... I didn't know what else to do, so I agreed."

As the soldiers prepared to depart, Armstrong asked if Brazel had examined the material. Brazel said that he studied it long enough to realize that "I don't what the hell it is." Armstrong replied, "We would rather you didn't talk very much about it."

In *Crash at Corona*, Bill Brazel describes the strange debris as falling into three categories. First, there was some material "on the order of balsa wood." Brazel tried whittling the wood-like material with his pocketknife but could not cut it in the least. Second, there was some string-like material that looked like "heavy-gauge monofilament fishing line." He tried breaking the filament and could not. Finally, there was a little piece of what looked like "tin foil." The foil-like material was, by far, the most interesting to Brazel. "I happened to notice when I put that piece of foil in that box and the damn thing just started unfolding and just flattened out! Then I go to playing with it. I'd fold it, crease it, lay it down and it'd unfold. It's kind of weird. I couldn't tear it."

In a presentation he gave at the 2nd Annual UFO Crash Retrieval Conference in 2004, Jesse Wade's son, Chuck, confirmed that after the Roswell crash, Bill Brazel showed up in his dad's bar. However, according to Chuck, not only did Brazel *talk* about the crash debris he had found, but he actually showed several pieces of the crash debris to interested bystanders. Patrons of the bar marveled at the strange properties of Brazel's material. This impromptu "show and tell" at Wade's Bar did not go unnoticed, and shortly thereafter, RAAF soldiers visited Bill Brazel at the Foster Ranch and took the pieces of debris away from him.

Chuck also remembers talking to Bill Brazel's brother, Vernon, about the strange debris found near Corona. "Bill's younger brother, Vernon, and I are about the same age. When

Vernon would come to town, he and I would play together. I can recall that we spoke about the UFO that crashed on the Foster Ranch."

As of this writing, the building in Corona, New Mexico that formerly housed Wade's bar is now abandoned. The building is located at 540 Main Street in Corona, and visitors may take photos from the street side. Please do not enter private property without obtaining the owner's permission in advance.

THIRTY:
ROSWELL: A BRIEF HISTORY
By John LeMay

Although thousands of tourists visit Roswell each year in search of information about UFOs, most of them know little of the area's rich history. Tourists typically visit the town's famous UFO museum and perhaps a few of the numerous gift shops along Main Street. As they walk and drive around town, unbeknownst to them, the story of Roswell's past screams out at them from the seemingly silent walls and interiors of many buildings and sites all around town. Prior to the publication of this book, few people knew exactly where to look for this spellbinding, hidden history. Now, contained herein are the resources needed to visit all the major historical sites related to the alleged UFO crash.

And, those of us interested in the rest of Roswell's history (before and after 1947) are certainly gratified when visitors who come looking for UFOs end up learning about the many fascinating aspects of the history of Southern New Mexico. In truth, the history of this part of New Mexico is deeply intertwined with all that is now considered *Americana* in U.S. history and beyond. Leaving the era of UFOs behind for a bit, let us turn back the calendar to discover how the town of Roswell came to be in the first place.

Traveling back in time to the late 1860s, we find that the area now called Roswell was mired in a period of Indian raids, unruly cowboys, dusty cattle drives and ruthless outlaws. Indeed, Southern New Mexico helped put the "wild" in the Wild West. Originally, the tiny settlement that became Roswell consisted of no more than a 15' x 15' adobe trading post and didn't even have an official name, being instead associated with the nearby Hispanic settlement of Rio Hondo. The trading post, built by James Patterson, was situated along the Goodnight-Loving Cattle Trail which was used to transport beef to the Indian reservation in Fort Sumner, New Mexico. Patterson's trading post was at an ideal spot along the way located in close approximation to several small rivers and an abundance of prairie grass.

Eventually, New England-born Van C. Smith came along and purchased Patterson's trading post, expanding the building and turning the establishment into a combination hotel, restaurant, saloon, and casino. Next door, he built a general store, which later became a post office. In 1873, needing a name for the post office, he chose "Roswell," which was his father's first name, and a town was born.

Smith would add another layer to Roswell's colorful Wild West past by turning his small settlement into a gambler's haven, a mini-Las Vegas, if you will, with round-the-clock card games, horse races, and even cockfights. Always seeking something new and more exciting, Smith soon left Roswell, putting the settlement in the hands of patriarchal southerner Captain Joseph C. Lea, a Civil War veteran who had ridden with Quantrill's Confederate Guerillas. Lea shut down the gambling and turned the town into a more respectable place, so much so that Roswell was even able to stay neutral in the Lincoln County War, New Mexico's biggest Wild West brouhaha.

The conflict was fought over cattle and land rights in Lincoln, now less than an hour's drive from modern day Roswell, and it consumed nearly all of Southeastern New Mexico in blazing gun battles and legal troubles. Captain Lea saw to it that no outlaws caused trouble in his town, most especially the notorious Billy the Kid. Many people are unaware of Roswell's close proximity to the events of the Lincoln County War, the story of which spawned several successful films such as *Young Guns I & II* with Emilio Estevez as Billy the Kid, Sam Peckinpah's *Pat Garrett and Billy the Kid* with James Coburn and Kris Kristofferson, and *Chisum* with John Wayne. Actually, Roswell was home to both John Chisum and Sheriff Pat Garrett, both regarded as heroes in the Lincoln County War.

John Simpson Chisum was one of the wealthiest cattle barons in the West. He came to the Roswell area in the late 1860s with several thousand head of cattle and eventually set up a ranch south of town which has stayed in operation in one way or another to this very day.

164

Pat Garrett moved to Roswell at the behest of Chisum and Captain Lea to run for Sheriff of Lincoln County, which at that time included the town of Roswell. Although the violence of the Lincoln County War had been stopped thanks to President Rutherford B. Hayes's threatening the territory with martial law, trouble was on the rise: cattle rustling at the hands of young desperados such as Billy the Kid. Garrett, who ironically had been Billy's gambling buddy in Ft. Sumner, won the bid for sheriff and tracked down the Kid and killed him in Ft. Sumner on July 14, 1881. There, Garrett took the Kid by surprise and shot him in a darkened room, thus making Garrett New Mexico's version of Wyatt Earp, in a sense, since he rid the West of one of its most feared outlaws.

Billy the Kid (left) and Pat Garrett (right), Courtesy of Wikipedia

Until the Roswell UFO story became popular in the late 1970s, the legacy of Billy the Kid, Pat Garrett, and the Lincoln County War had been the primary tourist attraction in Southern New Mexico. Ironically, there is actually a bizarre historical link between the Roswell Incident and the Lincoln County War. Sheriff Pat Garrett was shot and killed by a man named Jesse "Wayne" Brazel, who, as it turns out, was related to William "Mack" Brazel, the rancher who claimed to have found UFO debris at his

Lincoln County ranch in 1947. Some say Jesse was Mack's uncle, whereas others claim he was a second cousin.

Before being shot by Brazel in 1908, Garrett had a positive effect on the cultivation of the Roswell area with the help of Captain Lea. It was Garrett's idea to irrigate the Pecos Valley with large scale irrigation ditches branching off from several rivers. Although someone other than Garrett ended up finishing the project, Garrett's idea inevitably brought the railroad to Roswell. As happened in many other towns, the coming of the railroad, and later the telephone, heralded the end of the Old West.

While Garrett's partner, Charles Eddy, was away in Colorado looking for partners for their water venture, Eddy met wealthy Canadian John James Hagerman, a railroad man. Hagerman agreed to invest in Eddy's water-scheme, thus displacing Garrett, and came to visit Roswell. Upon arriving Hagerman decided that Roswell could use the services of a railroad and work got under way immediately. Roswell, which for a time claimed to be further from a railroad than any town in the West, finally greeted the arrival of its first locomotive in 1894. In a sense, Garrett helped bring about the modernization of the Old West in more ways than one, even though he may not have been aware of it at the time.

Roswell's growth continued through the early 20th century with few notable events of historical significance, until the arrival in town of pioneering rocket scientist Robert Hutchings Goddard. When Goddard's explosive rocket experiments incurred the wrath of his neighbors back in his native Massachusetts, famed aviator Charles Lindbergh suggested that Goddard might find the vast stretches of uninhabited desert around Roswell ideal for testing his rockets. Once in New Mexico, Goddard and his wife Esther set up their headquarters at Eden Valley, just north of Roswell -- coincidentally not far from the alleged final impact site of Roswell's crashed saucer in 1947.

While in Roswell, Goddard found weather conditions perfect for his rocket tests, and the locals, for the most part, tolerated his quirky experiments. Goddard's rocket tests in Roswell would have far reaching effects, extending literally to the moon and, before that, into London, England.

Robert H. Goddard (NASA Photo)

After unsuccessful attempts by Goddard to interest the U.S. military in his rocket technology, his plans were stolen by German spies, leading to the creation of the Nazi's V-2 rocket program. Only after the Germans used Goddard's rocket designs to rain down destruction upon London did the U.S. see the potential of rockets as weapons of war. As World War II ended, the U.S. captured Goddard's designs back from the Germans, along with their scientists and their expertise, and American rocketry finally got off the ground. Later, Goddard's designs paved the way to man's voyage into outer space and finally to the moon. Unfortunately, Goddard did not live to see the space age, as he died of throat cancer in August 1945, shortly after hearing the news of atomic bombs being dropped on Japan.

The ushering in of the Atomic Age was something else that Roswell bore close witness to. On July 16, 1945, the flash of light from the world's first detonation of an atomic device could be seen all the way in Roswell, only about a two hour drive from the Trinity Site near Alamogordo. The "cover story" fed by the military to New Mexico residents was that a military weapons depot had exploded. Was this a foreshadowing of the kind of cover-up later used to silence reports of a crashed flying saucer near Roswell?

Enola Gay and its Pilot, Paul Tibbetts, Jr. (U.S. Air Force Photo)

In another touch of irony, the Boeing B-29 bomber *Enola Gay*, which dropped the atomic bomb on Hiroshima, and the entire 509th Bomb Unit, the world's first atomic bomb group, were transferred to the Roswell Army Air Field in November of 1945. The RAAF, which had only existed for about four years, suddenly became one of the most important military installations in the world by virtue of its atomic arsenal. It was during this critical period in history that the Roswell Incident took place in 1947.

Numerous books have been written about the Roswell UFO case, containing many different accounts and witness testimony. While this information is certainly of great value, there is also much to be gained by visiting and exploring the actual places where these mysterious events reportedly happened, as urged in the old adage, *"If only these walls could talk."* Fittingly, the book you now hold in your hands takes you on a fascinating tour of the city of Roswell from the perspective of the famous 1947 UFO event. Here, for the first time, is the story of every historic building and eerie site that plays an important role in the story of the Roswell Incident.

John LeMay, Author and Historian
Roswell, New Mexico

INDEX

173

UFO Crash on the Texas-Mexico Border!
Now Available at RoswellBooks.com

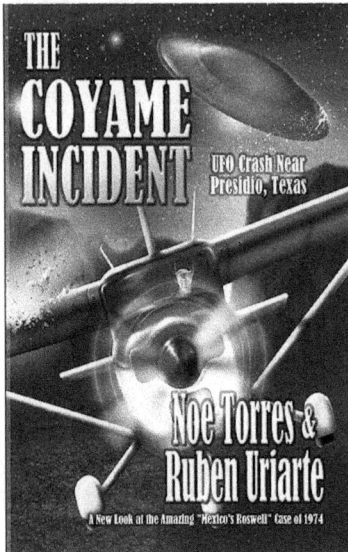

In this follow-up to their wildly-successful book, "Mexico's Roswell," the authors bring us up to date on the incredible story of a mid-air collision in August 1974 between a small plane and a UFO on the U.S.-Mexico border near the city of Presidio, Texas. Following the crash, the governments of both Mexico and the U.S. sent troops to recover the fallen UFO. Since the publication of their first book in 2007, the authors have uncovered several key new witnesses and a number of important new details about the case. This amazing UFO story has been featured on numerous television documentaries, including the History Channel's UFO Files, UFO Hunters, UFOs of the 1970s, and Extraterrestrial Contact.

Place your order today from Amazon.com, using the QR code shown.

The reviewers say: "Amazing! This story is wilder than the U.S. Roswell. This book is an amazing piece of work." – George Noory, Coast to Coast AM.

"The way you tell the story is very exciting, a great read. The prose really moves along and keeps the reader on the edge of her seat. Great job guys! " – Elaine Douglass, MIT Graduate and Veteran UFO Investigator.

"Torres and Uriarte are to be commended for tackling such an important case, whose impact on ufology may only now be coming to light thanks to the research they have undertaken. A definite must-read." – MUFON UFO Journal.

UFO Crash on the Texas-Mexico Border
Now Available at RoswellBooks.com

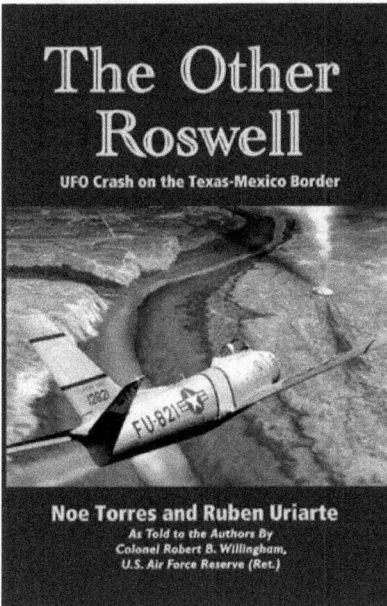

On a clear spring day in 1955, Air Force reservist Robert Willingham was piloting an F-86 fighter jet across West Texas when he saw an intensely bright UFO streak past his aircraft at over 2,000 miles per hour and then crash-land along the banks of the Rio Grande River, where he later found smoldering, twisted wreckage that convinced him the object was not of the Earth.

Dr. Bruce Maccabee, world-class UFO researcher, says about this book, "One of the world's most interesting UFO crash retrieval stories. I believe that the reader will find this book important support for the idea that Alien Flying Craft have crashed on earth and have been retrieved and covered up by the United States government."

The Other Roswell: UFO Crash on the Texas-Mexico Border discloses for the first time ever, the eyewitness testimony of Colonel Willingham, who says that he chased a UFO across Texas, saw it crash to the earth near Del Rio, Texas, and later visited the crash site.

You've heard about this amazing book on *Coast to Coast AM* with George Noory, the Jeff Rense program, and other shows we have done. Now, you can read the complete story from the eyewitness himself. Available for print and for the Kindle at RoswellBooks.com and through online retailers including Amazon.com. Scan the QR code here to order your copy from Amazon today!

Fallen Angel – Laredo UFO Incident
Now Available at RoswellBooks.com

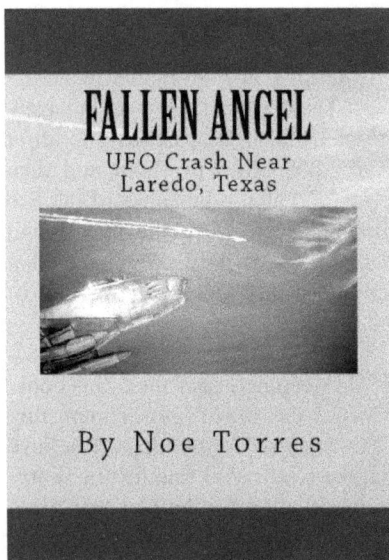

On July 7, 1948, U.S. military aircraft chased a fast-moving, 90-foot-diameter silver disc across Texas before watching it crash about 30 miles south-southwest of Laredo, Texas. Known as the "Laredo UFO Crash," this case occurred almost exactly one year after the famous Roswell UFO Incident and holds much of the same mystery and intrigue.

Witnesses later claimed that the military recovered a "fallen angel," a crashed alien ship and at least one non-human occupant.

For the first time ever, this book presents all of the evidence regarding this hotly-debated UFO case. First unveiled at the Laredo UFO Conference held on November 5, 2011 at Texas A & M International University, this book contains one of the least-known but most impressive UFO stories ever.

Author Noe Torres has appeared on the History Channel's "UFO Hunters," George Noory's "Coast to Coast AM," the Jeff Rense Program, and many other shows. His previous books include the widely-acclaimed "The Real Cowboys & Aliens: UFO Encounters of the Old West", "Ultimate Guide to the Roswell UFO Crash", and "Mexico's Roswell." He is currently director of the Mutual UFO Network (MUFON) in South Texas.

Available at RoswellBooks.com and through online retailers including Amazon.com. Scan the QR code above to order your copy from Amazon today!

RoswellBooks.com